DISRUPTIVE RESEARCH

Discover unmet user needs that drive revolutionary innovations

By Larry Marine

Disruptive Research: Discover unmet user needs that drive revolutionary innovations.

By Larry Marine.
Partially ghostwritten by Debbie Levitt.
Editors are listed at the end of the book.
Cover by Mallika Fraser [https://linkedin.com/in/mallikapf/].

LEGAL STUFF:

- WinAmp® is a registered trademark of AudioValley SA

- Finder®, iPod®, Apple Store®, iTunes®, and Apple Pay® are registered trademarks of Apple, Inc.

- FedEx Print® is a registered trademark of FedEx Office Managed Print Services

- FedEx Office® is a registered trademark of FedEx Print & Ship Services, Inc.

- American Airlines® is a registered trademark of American Airlines, Inc.

- Delta Airlines® is a registered trademark of Delta Airlines, Inc.

- JetBlue® is a registered trademark of JetBlue Airways Corporation.

- Google Maps® and Google Wallet® are registered trademarks of Google, LLC

- Marriott® is a registered trademark of Marriott International

Book Edition v1.0
First Edition/Printing: August 2023
Published by Delta CX Media [https://DeltaCX.Media]. ISBNs for this book are available on the Delta CX Media website.

Dedication

Over the years, clients and other practitioners have encouraged me to share my rather uncommon, yet successful, research and design methods. This book is dedicated to all of you for motivating me to complete this difficult task.

I especially want to offer my heartfelt thanks to Debbie Levitt, one of the most authentic and low-ego action heroes I've ever known. Her logic and wisdom kept me focused on writing a book that helps other practitioners evolve their skills. If it weren't for her guidance, this book would probably never have been completed. Thank you, Debbie.

Preface

Welcome! This book is focused on methods that might be new to you and different from how you do things now. These methods have been responsible for creating 10%-25% ecommerce conversion rates, creating new industries, setting the gold standard for entire industries, and generally disrupting markets. Disruptive Research is based on knowledge-oriented research and design techniques that are fresh, while also being tested and proven over decades.

Very different methods lead to very different results. Following these methods, you will discover research insights your company has been missing and will create designs that look little or nothing like your competition.

At first, this might seem scary or strange, since teams often sleepwalk straight into designs that look like what's already out there. If your company wants innovation, disruption, and to leap past the competition, then you must do just that.

Trust this process and your usability testing to give you the courage to move forward with the resulting revolutionary designs.

About Larry Marine

Larry Marine started his UX career after graduating from Dr. Don Norman's Cognitive Science program at UC San Diego where he learned the basic principles and processes of User-Centered Design (UCD). Don suggested that Larry become a Research and Design consultant, and Larry took that advice.

Since then, Larry has evolved these processes applying his experiences on over 250 projects with American Airlines, Vanguard Mutual Funds, FedEx, ProFlowers, Novartis, and more. He's had extraordinary results for decades in almost every domain, including medical, defense, enterprise, consumer products, ecommerce websites, and more.

Larry credits his experiences as a Navy computer tech for teaching him to solve for the root cause, not just the symptoms. He learned that if you don't accurately define the problem, the best you can hope to do is solve the wrong problem very well.

This book contains Larry's stories, methods, and experiences. He is the "I" in this book.

About Debbie Levitt

Debbie Levitt, MBA, is the CXO of Delta CX, and since the mid-1990s has been a Customer Experience (CX) and User Experience (UX) consultant focused on strategy, research, training, and Human-Centered Design (HCD)/User-Centered Design (UCD). She's a change agent and business design consultant focused on helping companies of all sizes transform towards customer-centricity while using principles of Agile and Lean.

She has worked in various CX and UX leadership and individual contributor roles at companies including Wells Fargo, Macy's, StepStone, Sony Mobile, and Constant Contact. In the 2010s, San Francisco UX and marketing agencies had Debbie on speed email. She completed projects for Traction, Fjord, LIFT, Rauxa, ROI·DNA, and Fiddlehead.

Clients have given her the nickname, "Mary Poppins," because she flies in, improves everything she can, sings a few songs, and flies away to her next adventure.

Her 2022 book, *Customers Know You Suck*, is the customer-centricity how-to manual. Start investigating what's holding you back from improving customer-centricity. Learn how to be value-led: how much value we can frequently create for potential and current customers.

You can also catch her on two YouTube channels, "Customer Experience – Customer Centricity" and "Delta CX".

Download the PDF of Images

Many of you will want access to the images in this book in a format where you can zoom in and see more detail. Please visit https://deltacx.link/dr-images for all of the images and examples herein.

Table of Contents

PART 1: WHAT IS DISRUPTIVE RESEARCH?

Chapter 1: Introduction

ProFlowers Sells Occasions

In the late 1990s, the executives of the ecommerce site ProFlowers® commissioned my consultancy, Intuitive Design, to design a new approach to buying flowers online. Florist websites across the internet were suffering from low conversion rates. ProFlowers' executives needed something innovative that would disrupt the market. They thought innovative ideas would be found by asking me to conduct usability tests on their competitors' websites, not realizing that copying competitors was far from innovating.

While visiting those websites, my team noticed that they were all very similar to each other. These sites were designed around the way the florists saw their business and all of them asked customers to build their own bouquets. "Florists build bouquets, so let's have users build bouquets." To innovate, the design would have to move past this approach.

Instead of running tests on competitors' websites, my team visited brick-and-mortar flower shops to observe how people bought flowers in the real world. They wanted to better understand users' cognitive processing behaviors rather than learning how they struggled with a poorly-designed website.

It quickly became obvious why online florists were suffering; *they were solving the wrong problem very well.* All of the existing florist sites expected users to combine various flowers to create floral bouquets. The problem was that most people buying flowers were men, who generally knew very little about flowers beyond thinking that roses were perfect for every occasion.

In the flower shops, the team observed that male customers typically demonstrated the same behaviors; they wouldn't ask the clerk for a specific bouquet with specific flowers, such as lilies and daffodils, they simply said, "I'm in trouble. I forgot my wife's birthday. What's a good bouquet to say I'm sorry?"

Florist websites were designed around the assumption that users had floral knowledge and knew how to build a bouquet, but they didn't. However, users do know what occasion the bouquet is for. Men weren't there for the flowers; they were there for a reason or an occasion.

The UX strategy became obvious: **ProFlowers doesn't sell flowers; they sell occasions.**

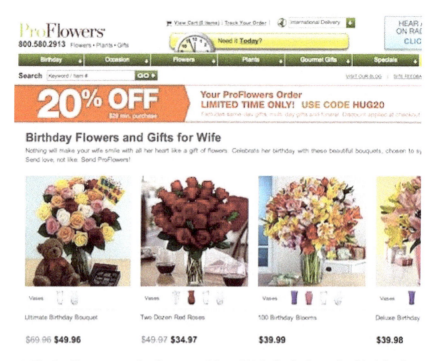

Figure 1: The ProFlowers.com landing page (circa 2014) displaying a few birthday bouquets.

The ProFlowers homepage design shows bouquets by occasion. In this screenshot, the category is, "Birthday Flowers and Gifts for Wife."

The new site was redesigned to eliminate the knowledge requirement of which flowers go well with others or which flowers match the situation or occasion. Rather than asking people to build or choose random bouquets, the design approach focused on organizing the site around occasions. Shoppers knew *why* they needed flowers, but not which flowers they needed. The redesigned system allowed users to choose the occasion, and be presented with a selection of bouquets perfect for that occasion.

The Accidental A/B Test

ProFlowers launched their new site just in time for Valentine's Day in 1998. A few weeks later, the ProFlowers executives called and wanted my consultancy to refund their money. "The new site is a miserable failure!"

I reviewed the new site, and noted obvious deviations from my team's original designs. A quick conference call confirmed our suspicions; the developers admitted that the occasion-oriented design didn't look like the competitors' sites, so they took the liberty of changing our design to make the site look just like other online florists. The executives were livid and told the developers to rebuild the site following our design.

They rebuilt the site following the design specifications, and relaunched in time for Mother's Day 1998. Since then, the site has been a top 10 ecommerce site. An average ecommerce site converts at around 2%. ProFlowers.com converted at over 25% every month for 20 years.

I was once mocked during a conference presentation for using design examples that were from the 1990s. I asked if anyone knew of designs that had performed as well for 20 years, 10 years, or even 2 years. *Crickets. No replies.*

The ProFlowers example is one of many that demonstrates the power of observational research and knowledge-oriented UX design.

Knowledge-Oriented UX, the Basis of Disruptive Research

More than just traditional UX done better or faster, knowledge-oriented UX is a more accurate method of defining the user's problem and helping to solve it. This book focuses on how to improve user observations and apply actionable insights to create market-dominating, disruptive designs that solve users' unmet needs.

While most UX tasks are tactical, knowledge-oriented UX is a strategic process that will be explained in more depth throughout the book:

- **Knowledge-oriented user research**. More than just doing research, it's about specifically learning how to identify unmet user needs. "Correctly defining the problem" is at the core of a variety of UX and design processes, but we must do more than just going through the motions or trying to boil something down to short exercises. There is no substitute for deeply understanding target users' tasks, needs, and problems.

- **Identifying the right UX strategy**. How to build the bridge between research insights and product design decisions. In this book, you will learn how to craft a UX strategy that is much more than a typical problem statement. The right strategy guides all of the subsequent design decisions towards a common goal.

- **Knowledge design**. Embedding knowledge identified through research—or already internal to your company—into the design makes your users more successful even when users' domain knowledge is limited.

There's never a wrong time to use this approach, but you will especially want to employ it when:

- Your current designs are not achieving the desired results, or you're not meeting metrics or Key Performance Indicators (KPIs).

- Customer satisfaction is low, stagnant, or dropping, and you need to act.

- Disrupting, innovating, or dominating your market is one of your strategic objectives.

- You've realized that you can't lead your market by ripping off competitors or playing competitor catch-up. You can't lead by following.

Process Overview

Our strategic process consists of the following phases (described in great detail throughout the book):

1. **Generative user research.** Research is the key to market-dominating UX success stories. Start with generative research to make sure that user problems are accurately defined and understood.

   o This research must occur in *every* project, whether your product is unknown, brand-new, or legacy.

   o This research focuses mostly on observing and interviewing people, but, similar to service design, also examines and maps systems, processes, relationships, and user contexts.

   o While we will use the term "generative research," you might also hear it referred to as "exploratory research" or "discovery."

2. **Task analysis and user knowledge profiles.** Task analysis more accurately identifies the problems the users are trying to solve and the hurdles that inhibit them. Rather than creating personas and then journey maps representing each persona's path, the knowledge-oriented UX process includes an analysis of the tasks that users perform to achieve their desired outcome as well as a more detailed user description focusing on user knowledge.

   o This involves creating detailed flow diagrams of the users' tasks, offering details and benefits that traditional customer journey maps and Jobs To Be Done diagrams miss.

   o Task analysis identifies users' problems from a solution-agnostic perspective. We are not yet considering or selecting any particular solutions, features, or designs, just understanding the steps they perform.

   o This phase generates user descriptions, which are referred to as user knowledge profiles, after some task analysis. These user knowledge profiles differ from personas and are explained later in the book.

3. **Task optimization.** This final phase of task analysis is the key to developing innovative approaches to solving users' problems. Optimizing the task flow identifies opportunities of where to embed task knowledge into the product to reduce the reliance on user skill and knowledge.

   o Optimization is not just polishing up the existing flow, and usually results in completely *changing* the flow. To some degree, this is the first step in "designing" the product.

- Optimizing the task leads to creating flow diagrams of the improved future state interactions, interfaces, and experiences. It focuses on identifying ways to make the system do more of the work for the users, rather than the other way around.

4. **Prioritization.** Prioritization ensures that the team focuses the UX design energy on what will deliver the most user value. This is a straightforward method to get consensus, and identify which tasks are the highest priority to solve from the users' viewpoint.

   - Prioritization utilizes three key perspectives: user needs, business objectives, and the technical feasibility of addressing the perceived requirements.

   - The result is a priority or viability matrix that suggests a roadmap of which tasks to solve now and later.

5. **Defining the UX design strategy.** The "aha!" moment in task analysis and optimization comes by identifying an overarching strategy that will guide the design effort. Analyzing the task recognizes that users are trying to achieve a specific goal in a certain way, and that a specific strategy—distinct from current designs—would suit them best. This strategy becomes more evident as the analysis progresses.

   - Strategies are not defined by KPIs, such as "increase sales by 5%." They are an overarching solution approach related to the problem, a guiding statement of *what* to achieve, not *how* or *by how much*. For example, the ProFlowers strategy was "ProFlowers doesn't sell flowers. They sell occasions."

6. **Knowledge design.** This is a key step that isn't widely described in other UX methodologies. Rather than simply adding controls or instructions to a screen, knowledge design focuses on how to utilize a company's knowledge about the domain—plus what we learned from research—to reduce user effort.

   - User knowledge profile descriptions created during the task analysis phase identify knowledge gaps that can be "filled" by the design to reduce dependencies on individual levels of user skill and knowledge.

   - Typically, the task optimization identifies *where* knowledge needs to be embedded, useful when creating the product design.

7. **Task-oriented design.** Rather than creating a set of features on a single screen, focus on providing a set of screens that follow the optimized task flow and provide just the right features on each screen to match the steps of the task flow. It's perfectly acceptable and recommended to reuse a feature on other screens for other tasks.

  o For example, a website might reuse the same feature in all three of its main tasks, but slightly differently for each task based on the specific needs of that task.

8. **Usability testing.** This evaluative research is justifiably a staple of HCD. No matter how well you think you've created your design, the users will always prove you wrong. Get used to learning through small and large failures. Embrace them. Plan for them. You will need to test, improve, iterate, and test again.

Avoid Gut Instincts

I have several top-performing designs that have withstood the test of time, a testament to the success of the knowledge-oriented UX methods that are described in this book. The key aspect of these processes and this book is the importance of accurately defining the problem you need to solve for your users.

Not all of my projects have been successful. Some clients deliberately chose to avoid good research to "go with their gut." Sadly, those projects suffered shameful fates, ending up in the landfill of failed designs and disaster projects.

These failures tend to have a familiar pattern: A stakeholder presents their perspective on a challenge, question, or new project, and we rejoice that we now have a problem to work on. But do we have a *good* understanding of the *right* problem? These stated "problems" are often not the real problem, but symptoms of larger or other problems. To avoid falling into the trap of focusing on the symptoms, we must more accurately define the problem.

"If you don't accurately define the problem, the best you can hope to do is solve the wrong problem very well."—Larry Marine

---

It's faster and easier to perform simplified or no research than to conduct *good* user research. Teams are often obsessed with the speed of the project over the effectiveness of the solution. Many teams conduct inaccurate or incorrect user research, which unsurprisingly leads to inaccurate and incorrect problem definitions.

The only time UX is lightning fast is when we are cutting corners or doing it somewhat wrong.

PART 2:   GENERATIVE USER RESEARCH

Chapter 2:   Research Methods

The best solutions come from the best problem definitions. The most accurate problem definitions come from unbiased generative research. Of all the research methods commonly available, direct observational research provides the most objective generative insights. Many other research methods typically suffer from self-reporting biases that adversely affect the research.

Knowing which method to use is just as important as conducting the research. The strategic choices ensure more accurate insights, leading to a more successful design. Choosing the right method depends on several factors, including:

- **Is this a redesign or improvement of an existing design?** A redesign is more proactive and innovative; observational research is much more objective and would be a good strategy. Improving an existing design is more reactive and incremental; interviewing or usability testing are good options for that route.

- **Is the intent to move into a new market or expand an existing market?** Observational research or contextual interviews would help identify the needs of a new or expanding market. This relies on a more proactive approach.

- **Are we fixing problems with an existing product or feature?** Usability testing is best suited to answer this question. This is a more reactive effort.

The following graph compares which research methods lead to reactive vs. proactive insights. Reactive insights are derived from a user reacting to a given design versus proactive, which refers to understanding the problem before a solution even exists. The graph measures their effectiveness as being either more incremental (improving an existing design) or more innovative (coming up with a completely new design approach).

Caveat: this is not a scientifically accurate measure, but it does reflect 30 years of experience conducting various types of research.

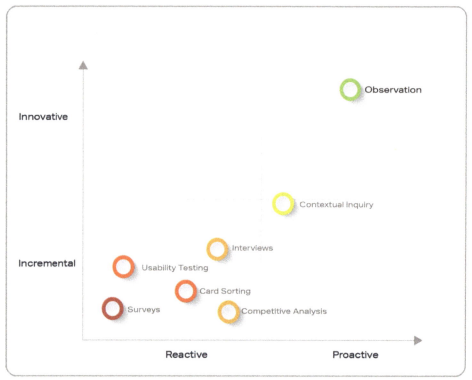

Figure 2: A 2 × 2 chart depicting the approximate applicability of some common research methods.

This 2 × 2 chart indicates the applicability of seven research methods measured on a scale of incremental to innovative on one axis, and reactive to proactive on the other axis. This roughly suggests that:

- Surveys tend to be more incremental and reactive.

- Competitive analysis is equally as incremental, but not as reactive.

- Card sorting is a little less incremental, but still reactive.

- Usability testing is midway in the incremental range, but highly reactive.

- Interviews are toward the middle of the chart, but lean toward incremental and reactive.

- Contextual inquiry is in the middle of the chart, midway between incremental and innovative, as well as midway between reactive and proactive.

- Observation is very innovative and proactive.

If the objective is to polish an existing design, reactive user feedback, such as surveys or usability testing, can be part of your research. However, if the objective is to innovate, surveys and usability testing won't provide the insights that more proactive observational research will.

Generative vs. Evaluative Research

There are basically two different kinds of user research. **Generative** is about discovering new insights or opportunities, often through observations and interviews. The best generative research is solution-agnostic and not focused on any idea, solution, or design. This allows researchers to accurately identify user behaviors, unmet needs, and insights.

Evaluative research methods incrementally improve concepts or designs, often through usability testing. As evaluative user feedback is typically limited to reactions to an existing design, it typically fails to provide revolutionary insights that fundamentally change a product or design. It does, however, provide quick-fix insights for existing designs, which is sometimes the only feasible approach available.

Using the ProFlowers example, the project started with generative research: observing buyers in actual flower shops. The team didn't evaluate or usability test existing florist websites, nor did they spend time on competitive analyses.

These observations uncovered the key design strategy that propelled ProFlowers to the top of the online florist market. Usability testing existing websites would not have uncovered the key unmet need that transformed online florist design approaches; it would have only led to incrementally improving the wrong design, and putting lipstick on the pig.

Unbiased Generative Methods

Unbiased generative methods reveal more about user behaviors, needs, and tasks than self-reporting methods or quantitative methods.

Observation is the most successful and accurate method, but it is also the most difficult to accomplish correctly. The hard part is making sure that the researchers can actually observe the desired events without having to artificially manufacture a trigger event, something familiar to the user that initiates the desired task. For example, "Is that funny noise that the refrigerator is making a problem or not?" The trigger is the very first thought or event that sparks the task.

The observation must be as natural as possible. Any contrived scenario removes some of the inherent motivations and changes the users' behaviors. For example, bringing users into a research lab removes people from their environment and equipment, and this will artificially influence their behaviors.

Contextual inquiry. In their seminal work, *Contextual Design: Defining Customer Centered Systems*, Hugh Beyer and Karen Holtzblatt describe how to perform an observational research method. The method involves observing users in their actual work settings using a product, and then interviewing them afterwards.

This is a common generative research method, but it does have an inherent weakness that you must try to avoid. When focusing on observing users using the current product, the implicit assumption is that the current product is the right product approach or starting point. Historically, the existing product is rarely the right solution for users or their tasks. The current product is typically a legacy product that didn't benefit from good user research, or was copied from a competitor (who probably didn't do good user research either).

Conducting contextual inquiry on an existing product can incrementally improve the existing design, but it doesn't necessarily identify innovative insights. You get the most insightful results by conducting contextual inquiry in a more solution-agnostic, task-oriented manner. This helps avoid the bias towards the existing solution and provides better insights that help define the root cause of the problem.

This process takes some practice to reach the point where the researcher can remain solution-agnostic, separating the tasks from the tools, to identify ground-breaking innovative insights. Being solution-agnostic means avoiding focusing on a specific technology or solution, and not trying to prove or disprove an existing idea or design. Using an existing design typically limits the users' behaviors and suggestions to only those supported by or related to the design.

If possible, observe users in a task environment that either does not use a specific technology, or observe them using a variety of technologies. For example, rather than observing people shop for shoes online, visit a shoe store and observe the users' actions and decision-making processes. The goal is to learn how they do this now, whether or not that includes a particular system or tool.

Why Use Observational Research over Other Methods?

It's discouraging to hear so-called data-driven executives try to dissuade researchers from "bothering" with observational research. The common complaint is that they feel they already know their users and their problems, and therefore don't need to invest the time and money that good generative research requires. Yet, when observational research is done well, executives, teammates, and others are surprised by the insights and opportunities because it uncovers data they didn't already know or have.

Observational research is not as easy to perform as user interviews and other methods because the researcher is looking for the invisible, unspoken, or missing element of a users' problem or task rather than what they say or write down.

For example, a user may briefly glance at a sticky note without actually using the information on it. Why would they do that? It might be that the note did not have the information they were looking for. Asking what they were looking for would be a point of interest to ask about during the post-observation interview.

The researcher must be a detective. Not everybody is a great researcher, and not everybody is a great detective. These are specialized skills that researchers sharpen over years.

Chapter 3:   Improving Observational Research Skills

Conducting user observations well enough to uncover unseen and unspoken disruptive insights is the key to accurately defining or redefining the problems our users have, whether or not they are aware of these problems. Simple acts of observing and documenting design ideas, or "getting feedback," rarely uncovers ideas that disrupt a market.

The key to good observational research is to remain open-minded and objective. It's those unexpected insights that drive great ideas and products. Remain disciplined and observe the users before rushing headlong into design or solution brainstorming.

Where to Start

Researchers often mistakenly start by examining the current solutions or those from the competitors. This assumes that these solutions are right or good, or solve the right problems. Too many designs are a regurgitation of other existing designs, or were "inspired by" competitive analyses, examining the solutions other companies chose. This approach falsely assumes that the other designs are good enough and solve the right problems.

That's not to say that competitive analysis isn't a useful method; it's just not a starting point for generative qualitative research. Great observational research will identify other problems, including ones outside of what existing solutions attempt to solve.

Don't start with predetermined hypotheses that can unintentionally drive the results to fit into "the box" suggested by the hypothesis. Instead, start by trying to understand what triggers users to start their task, and the steps of the tasks that users perform to achieve their desired outcome.

> The inherent failure of a competitive analysis is that there is no guarantee that the competitors did the right research and solved the right problem.

For example, when beginning a typical dashboard design project, consider that a dashboard may not be the right solution. Start the research by asking these types of questions:

- What are the users trying to identify?

- Which actions does the product need to suggest to achieve the users' desired outcomes?

- What will it take to drive those actions?

- How can the new product support or perform those actions for the user?

Challenge existing assumptions and look for unmet needs beyond the existing solutions. Look at the whole task from beginning to end, not just the part that the current solutions focus on. Start with what triggers the user to take action, what their desired outcome is, and all of the steps that achieve that outcome.

Research the Domain

When preparing to observe or interview users in complex task environments, it helps to research the domain to develop an understanding of the nuances and complexities of that task domain. If the users think the researcher doesn't know much about the domain, they will alter and simplify their language to make it easier for the researcher to understand. This colors the interaction and hinders the ability to uncover insights.

By knowing enough to ask intelligent, domain-specific questions, the researcher can develop a peer-level conversation with the users that can uncover key insights. This is where Subject Matter Experts (SMEs) can really help. Conversations with SMEs prior to conducting the observations can provide the necessary foundation to help you understand the domain well enough to notice nuances that lead to useful insights.

Subject Matter Experts are invaluable resources but are often used incorrectly. The common practice is to rely on the SMEs to define the problem, but sometimes they are not representative users. They typically know much more about the problem domain than real users; this often biases the problem definition towards the SMEs' experience, opinions, or assumptions. Some SMEs have business experience in the domain but lack hands-on user experience with the task. For example, a SME might describe the problem as if all users were savvy or experts, which they are not.

They can give some insight into a potential best practice, or some fundamental understanding of a process, but SMEs are not that useful to observe as users. They know too much and tend to do things that justify an existing design (that they likely helped design). Moreover, they do things differently than the average user.

One of the most effective uses of SMEs' expertise is to ask them questions about your observations. When you don't understand an observed behavior, the SME is often able to provide insightful details.

Planning Observational Research

In-person observations are the most objective methods for gaining truly insightful knowledge about the users' perception of their tasks and associated behaviors.

Understanding the task domain might suggest how to best observe the users in their natural task environment.

With in-person observations, avoid getting in the user's way and try to determine where the researchers should locate themselves in the task environment. Find a spot that provides a clear view of the task environment without interrupting the user's activity flow. This often requires that you first gain insight into what the expected flow might be, allowing you to plan what the observation routine might require. I'll cover how to pilot the observation shortly.

Bringing users into a conference room to observe them using an app or website removes all of their external artifacts, changes their natural behavior, and reduces their comfort level. It is better to observe them in their typical environment.

Another consideration when planning the observation is the number of researchers to invite. I recommend no more than three researchers in one work location or station. If there are several stations to observe, then you can post one to three researchers at each station. More than three researchers tend to overwhelm the users.

Recording User Observations

One way to capture observations is by video recording or taking photographs of participants from one or more angles. Videos or photos can provide insights for events that are difficult to anticipate or control, or that occur over a protracted length of time.

However, videos also come with potentially prohibitive costs. They demand a lot of time to review, and the camera can miss small details. Most cameras typically point in just one direction and miss events occurring out of view. Setting up multiple cameras demands a lot of time and dramatically increases the time required to review and synthesize the observations from the various angles.

Privacy, security, or other legal issues might prohibit video recording. If your project involves tasks occurring in a workplace, you may be able to use existing security camera footage to observe some tasks. Many workplaces have security or safety surveillance cameras installed. One limitation of security video is that it may not capture the necessary detail or may be focused on one area and may miss triggers or artifacts in other areas of the workspace.

Where cameras can run automatically or be remotely controlled and don't have researchers behind them, users quickly grow accustomed to the camera and eventually forget it's there, allowing them to perform and act naturally. Users tend to interact with a camera operator or observer in the room with them, which biases the observations.

Always check to see if user consent is required. If so, be sure to get consent before recording people. Typically, individual users such as consumer website users require consent forms. Workplace projects are more likely to prohibit recording, but if they allow recording, they usually don't require individual consent forms. If in doubt, it's better to provide one.

Pilot the Observation

If possible, arrange a practice observation that allows the research team to gain an understanding of the typical task flow. In one blood analyzing research project, the researchers familiarized themselves with the blood analyzing process by interviewing a Subject Matter Expert to walk the team through the typical laboratory process, highlighting potential points of interest in the task flow.

It isn't necessary to use actual representative users for the practice observations. The objective is to gain some perspective on the task environment to identify any potential issues or important observations to focus on. Piloting the observation technique with internal lab techs in the company lab, even though they weren't exactly representative (they knew too much about the product), helped ensure that the researchers would have some common knowledge about which kinds of actions to look for and how to avoid getting in the users' way.

This pilot observation also helped ensure that each researcher would provide similar data across all of the observations. The team reviewed the practice observation technique and discussed what kind of information they might see, and which elements are important to capture.

If internal users are not available for piloting the observations, it's acceptable to recruit actual users (even if they are not exactly representative); they will need to be compensated just as the other users will be. Do not expect to use the data collected in these pilot observations. There will likely be interruptions when researchers ask questions about the process, and this invalidates the objectivity of the observations. The pilot observation is more about familiarizing the observation team with the process, not collecting user data, and therefore it's fine if the data is not necessarily viable.

Remote Observations: A Common Limitation

Many researchers must or choose to conduct remote screen-sharing as their main observation technique. Granted, this is often the only feasible way to observe the users' behavior, but too many research efforts rely on remote observations out of expediency rather than necessity, even when in-person observations are possible.

Remote observation is biased by the websites, software, or apps that the user uses to perform their task. The observations tend to be a reflection of how the user uses existing solutions, not how they actually want to do something.

Moreover, there are things to be observed outside of the screen-share that users employ in their tasks, such as sticky notes, note pads, and other external artifacts that affect the users' behaviors. These off-screen artifacts and actions are indicators of unmet user needs and often represent the most useful insights that drive true innovative designs.

Try to schedule in-person observations when feasible. Only use remote observation when necessary. If remote observation is the only available option, ask the participant if they can use their camera to briefly show their workspace, such as their desk, any notebooks or cheat sheets, any other technologies, or anything else they use during the task. This should give a better indication of what "knowledge" they use to help them with their task.

Observation Team Cadence

Time is often a guiding factor in the observation effort, and teams need to complete their observations as quickly as feasible. However, the team should schedule breaks in the observations to share their insights with each other. This gives a chance to surface any items that need further investigation or observation with subsequent participants.

This cadence should include a brief (5-10 minute) informal discussion after the first observation. This is not intended to be a formal meeting, but just a quick checkpoint discussion to share some observation insights. Consider holding another brief checkpoint discussion after a few more observations to again share some observation sights and evolve the observation techniques. These insights tend to include suggestions about what kinds of things to look for, how to observe something, any questions a researcher might have about the users, tasks, or domain. This is not a formal review. That will come later.

Number of Observations

The key to getting the most out of the observations is making sure that the observed users are a good representative sample of the target user-base. The more representative they are, the fewer participants you need to observe. If the observed users are truly representative of the typical user base, then the team will identify the most useful insights within eight to twelve observations per user group.

Some practitioners, such as the Nielsen Norman Group (NN/g), suggest that good enough results can be achieved testing with only three to five people per user group. Many practitioners have used this suggestion to inappropriately decrease the number of generative research participants as well. To be fair, NN/g suggested three to five people per user group for usability testing, which is a valid argument if you are only looking to find the most common 80%-90% of the design issues. As we care more and more about diversity and including people with disabilities or accessibility needs, it's best to update these older recommendations. At the very least, be sure to intentionally invite diverse users.

Your participants will essentially be speaking and acting for the target audience they are a part of. Therefore, we must make sure to meet with the correct number of the best audience representatives. This speaks directly to our recruiting and participant selection.

Testing with five users could give us around 85% of usability issues that affect 31% or more of the users (one-third of users); this heuristic is useful only when we:

1. Know who our users are.

2. Have users perform realistic closed-ended tasks with clear objectives.

3. Know that with five users we will only identify 85% of the more obvious problems (those affecting more than a third of all users) and just a few of the less obvious problems.

4. Change the users or tasks when we start over.

["Why You Only Need to Test with Five Users (Explained)," Jeff Sauro. March 8, 2010. https://measuringu.com/five-users/]

Whom to Observe

People often believe that the product's existing users are the best population to research. Although these are often the easiest users to find, they will not provide the insights that achieve disruptive designs. These customers have experience with your products and services. Some of them might be able to use your system with their eyes closed. They might already have workarounds and tricks that help your system seem better than it is.

The worst version of this is when a team recruits only for "happy" customers. If inviting existing customers, make sure to pick a few that have left poor satisfaction scores. That said, you can use existing customers only if they accurately represent your target user knowledge profile (more on that, later), but be careful to avoid any biases towards the existing solution.

Rather than recruiting for the easiest-to-find users, recruit people who accurately represent the target user knowledge profile. Here are some ways to try to find more appropriate research participants. Note that I recommend pulling from these groups only when the individuals match the target profiles, audience, or segments. **Use screener surveys to weed out anybody who isn't a match to the target user base.**

- **Potential customers**. These are some of the best users for observational research. They are part of the target audience, are familiar with the domain, and are intrinsically motivated. They might not have used the existing solution much or at all and may be interested in solving a problem in the product domain.

- **Former customers**. This is a hard group to get, as they have decided to not do business with the company any longer. However, a generous incentive could entice some of them. Partner with the sales team to get their suggestions on who to reach out to.

    o Note that this group also has existing familiarity and knowledge of the product, which will bias their perspective. Make sure they do not feel that this is an attempt at winning them back; this is purely research.

- **Conference attendees**. It helps to attend a conference where the target user types will likely be attending. For example, Debbie Levitt attended a real estate conference to speak to realtors about personal safety when they show houses.

- o I attended a blood screening conference to research a blood screening control software approach for lab directors. The conference was attended by nearly every large-scale blood screening lab director in the world. There were also plenty of vendors with blood screening equipment who offered conversations about problems in the blood screening arena.

- **Members of user groups and meetups**. These are great places to find users who have a relationship with the specific product domain. Attend a few meetings to connect with target users. Check with organizers to make sure they approve of you approaching members for a research study.

- **Participants found by market research companies or outside panel services**. These can be hit or miss. Since these people participate in research studies with some frequency, they are sometimes wise to what you are looking for and keen to deliver it. This could jeopardize or bias the research.

- **Family and friends (possibly only for pilot testing where results are not part of the final insights or report)**. These users may already be familiar with the design, but they can help you pilot test the observation plan.

- **Members of your church, faith, or religious group**. This is a user population that may be quite varied and may be easy to approach. There is some potential bias just because they are all part of the same group.

- **Random people met in coffee shops**. This can be acceptable when recruiting a more generic user knowledge profile, especially if you are not heavily screening for specific people or skills. Have a few preliminary questions prepared to weed people in or out so you don't bother observing the wrong audience.

  - o It also takes the right personality to approach people in a coffee shop without raising coffee drinkers' defenses or making the staff concerned that you're creepy. Try a shop where you're a regular and people recognize you, and speak to the staff to make sure they approve of your research activities. Be prepared to buy lots of coffee.

Keep in mind that, though these are good places to find potential participants, you still must qualify them with your participant screener.

Proxies: Alternative Users

Sometimes, you can observe similar users from another environment as a proxy for the target user and task. These are options to consider when finding target participants who can perform the desired tasks is difficult.

Try these alternate approaches:

- **Analogous scenarios**. It is very difficult to gain access to watch doctors perform certain medical procedures. Consider observing veterinarians performing a similar procedure on animals to learn more about the task. If it's problematic to watch a nurse performing a certain task, try observing a respiratory therapist or other specialist performing a similar task. These can still provide critical user insights not discoverable in any other way.

  o Finding an analogous task domain can be difficult. Be creative. Try looking outside of the domain altogether. For example, the process of making travel bookings has parallels to making large dinner party plans for visiting friends and family. Finding that perfect restaurant that pleases everybody could be close enough to give you ideas of the problems people face in looking for that perfect vacation spot.

- **Training scenarios**. When direct observations are not an option due to unpredictability of events, security or privacy issues, or other factors, it may be possible to observe relevant training scenarios. These scenarios commonly are not very representative of the actual events and can bias the problem definition, but they may be the only option available.

  o Unfortunately, the researcher won't be able to determine what is realistic and representative and what is not. Many training scenarios are not based on real-world tasks. Therefore, these might be an option, but choose carefully and watch for biases and moments that don't match real users' tasks.

- **Simulators** are another form of training that can closely replicate specific scenarios. Although some simulators are quite realistic, the users still know it's not real, and therefore have a different intrinsic motivation.

  o For example, rather than fearing for their lives in a real in-flight emergency, flight simulator users are focused on earning a score. These are very different motivators and alter the observed behaviors.

If no other options are available, proxies and alternative scenarios can be better than no observational research at all. Coupled with interviews of actual users of the intended tasks, this can still provide valuable insights into an otherwise unobservable task.

Look for "Task Dimensions" During the Observations

There are four key aspects of users' tasks that researchers should specifically look for during observational studies. These categories of observations are most likely to uncover new opportunities for the project or for the company in general. These indicate unmet needs that users would love to see addressed.

During observations, watch for task steps that are:

- Manually intensive.

- Cognitively demanding.

- Error prone.

- Knowledge dependent.

These are referred to as "Task Dimensions." The last one is the most important, since it leads directly to a knowledge-oriented design approach. During observations, Task Dimensions are often easier to spot when you notice the tools and workarounds the user has created or added to try to make the task easier or more successful. They include notes, pencils, books, maps, calculators, spreadsheets, applications, browser plug-ins, smartphone apps, reference books or manuals, and someone the user asks for help.

Take special note of these tools, workarounds, and artifacts since they will be mapped during the task analysis phase. We consider them during the knowledge design work; the new design needs to eliminate the need for these artifacts.

Don't replace tools and workarounds with instructions, tooltips, or tutorials. Make sure to solve root causes without automating existing solutions or creating Band-Aids® that are only an incremental improvement. Instead, use automation to replace user tasks rather than to merely automate an existing solution, such as making an app that mimics a spreadsheet. Such an app doesn't change the user's task; it just changes the tool they use.

"Instructions are a symptom, not a solution."—Larry Marine

To help explain Task Dimensions, let's use an example from one of my past projects. The Coast Guard's search-and-rescue planning of a sinking sailboat is quite complex. It started when a distress signal indicated a sailboat was sinking in the Atlantic Ocean. We observed several planners using large tables to lay out large maps of weather patterns, ocean currents, shipping lanes, aircraft routes, and more. They feverishly made numerous measurements with various tools. They often switched between these maps, wrote measurements down, made calculations, and typed results into a spreadsheet.

This evolution took several planners hours to perform, and was done while coordinating ad hoc search efforts with local resources, such as ships and aircraft passing by the projected location of the sinking vessel. All of these ships and passing aircraft were useful *assets* to aid in the search, but required a coordinated plan to avoid missing patches of ocean or wasting time by observing the same patch of ocean multiple times. This coordination was also complicated when new assets were added or existing assets left, such as when a passing freighter had to abandon their search efforts to go into port for more fuel.

Manually Intensive Tasks

Manually intensive tasks are typically very inefficient and not well optimized. There are many steps that one or more people must perform precisely. There is little or no automation.

In the Coast Guard example, the manually intensive tasks included finding the right maps, shifting between different maps, plotting the paths of existing assets (ships and airplanes), and making numerous measurements. These measurements were performed with various tools such as protractors, mapping combs, parallel nautical rulers, and calipers. The Coast Guard also used wind and tide charts as knowledge artifacts to help them with their manual tasks.

Cognitively Demanding Tasks

Some tasks demand greater cognitive processing, especially when users are trying to organize or solve parts of the task in their heads. Since we often don't like to think, tasks that demand more focused thought are common indicators of users' unmet needs.

Cognitively demanding steps require users to think, judge, and process. They need to remember many different things, but often forget or lose track. To offload this cognitive burden (the demand on the user's cognitive resources), users rely on tools and artifacts including instructions, notes, shortcuts, workarounds, tables, graphs, and other tools that exist outside of the product or service.

Using the Coast Guard example, the many calculations of wind, ocean currents, and shipping timetables demanded lots of cognitive processing in order to coordinate the rescue efforts.

In a typical cognitively demanding task step, the user does have the necessary knowledge but is burdened by the cognitive demands of the task. This is different from "knowledge dependent" steps where users don't have the requisite knowledge, and sometimes don't know what they don't know.

Error-Prone Tasks

If users commit errors during their task, try to ascertain whether the error-inducing aspect is due to a physical device, a cognitive burden issue, or something else. For example, when observing the usage of a medical device, one step was so cognitively demanding and prone to error that the researchers literally held their breath during the task to avoid interrupting the user. Any error would invalidate the entire process and the user would have to start over, destroying several patient samples in the process.

Also check if errors are happening enough to be predictable. For example, how often do you arrive on a form asking for your phone number, and you start to wonder how you'll get it wrong this time. You assume that your phone number entry won't match the website's desired format, and you'll get an error message. Date, phone number, and other formatted entries are common and predictable errors that users struggle with on websites.

The Coast Guard rescue planning process was rife with potential errors, which further increased the cognitive demand. Calculations might be incorrect, or someone might have misread a map. Lives were on the line, and no one wanted to make a mistake. This effort included several collaborators sharing calculations in handwritten notes, which are susceptible to comprehension and transposition errors.

Knowledge Dependencies

Most tasks have a basic knowledge requirement that average users can be expected to meet, called "common knowledge." Knowledge requirements that go beyond these expectations indicate knowledge that the users won't likely have, and highlight opportunities for improvement. This difference between the common knowledge users can be expected to know and the knowledge they will need to know **but won't** represent the knowledge gap that knowledge-oriented UX bridges.

> Users can only perform at a level no greater than their individual levels of skill and knowledge. Any design that relies on user skill and knowledge cannot promote user performance at a level greater than that highly variable skill and knowledge.

Look for common examples of artifacts that signal a knowledge dependency or lack of knowledge, including:

- **Notes**. Users can't remember some information that is important to the task. They might be aware of this and have left notes and cheat sheets for themselves.

- **Workarounds**. Workarounds are a clear indication that the design does not support the way users think about the task. For example, using a screenshot to capture data rather than using a cumbersome feature to upload a data set.

- **Guesses and low confidence**. If the user is guessing at what to do, slowing down, reading things more carefully, and hesitating, they might be lacking knowledge.

- **Deep thought.** The user often pauses while they try to remember or figure out if they know the required information. This is usually indicated by users becoming silent while they focus on the task.

- **Confidently wrong**. Debbie Levitt and I watched one participant confidently type "navy blue" in a form field asking for her Pantone color *number* for a logo. The system didn't give her an error message. The company will either guess at a Pantone color for her, or the company might delay her order to ask again for her logo's Pantone color number.

- **Instructions.** Tutorials, product tours, tooltips, instructional text, and videos signify that something isn't intuitive or easy to use, and will require training the users, who otherwise might not figure this out. A good task-oriented design will not require any of these design Band-Aids.

In the ProFlowers example, competitor websites required users to build bouquets, but the average flower buyer in this instance knows nearly nothing about individual flowers. They are even less likely to know the right flowers to combine into a bouquet. Providing occasion-based pre-designed bouquets eliminated that floral knowledge requirement.

The knowledge gap—between what users know and need to know but likely won't— is the fundamental basis of a knowledge-oriented design approach. Bridging that gap is what transforms a product or service company into a *knowledge company*, and leads to successful, if not disruptive, designs.

The Coast Guard operation demanded extensive knowledge around knowing which charts or maps to use, reading and interpreting them, calculating for wind drift and current flow, and the visibility range of various searching watercraft and planes. The users were all very familiar with reading the charts; not all were as familiar with calculating wind drift and current flow; and all made educated guesses about the visibility of the other watercraft and planes in the area. In essence, they lacked some key knowledge about the event (watercraft and planes) that could jeopardize the search efforts. Success relied on knowledge that the users were not likely to have.

Another Observation Example

One client asked us to analyze a product that provided monthly sales results data to pharmaceutical companies so they could track their sales representatives' successes. This was an indirect sales task domain; sales reps didn't actually sell pharmaceuticals to the doctors. They could only encourage the doctors to write prescriptions for their company's brand of an equivalent drug.

Unfortunately, the product did not give the sales reps the information they needed to improve their sales practices. The client provided the monthly sales data in a FedEx (courier) package, literally a ream of paper with rows and columns of various sales data sent to each sales rep. These sales reps were too busy meeting with their doctor customers to read and make sense of this data. We noticed many unopened sales report packages at sales reps' offices.

Our observations included watching some of the sales reps try to make sense of the rows and columns of data. It was far beyond their expertise; they had trouble understanding what the data meant and what to do differently. This was clearly a task domain with high cognitive demand and knowledge requirements.

Sales reps are motivated to reach specific sales targets in order to earn a bonus. The more they "sold," the greater their bonus. Observations of the sales managers identified that some sales managers had success formulas that routinely achieved bonus targets. Managers would encourage their reps to use these techniques to help them achieve their bonus, but this information was not codified within the company.

It turned out that of the hundred or so doctors each sales rep had in their region, 80% of sales were generated by just eight to ten doctors. Rather than visiting all of the doctors equally as often, focusing more attention on the top eight to ten doctors resulted in more sales and bigger bonuses.

This success formula was the company knowledge that bridged the sales rep knowledge gap. Rather than shipping out reams of data that were never read, we designed a single page graph that tracked their sales activities, which doctors they visited, and then suggested which doctors needed another visit (more about this, later).

Data vs. Graph

Which of the following two images would you expect to be more successful?

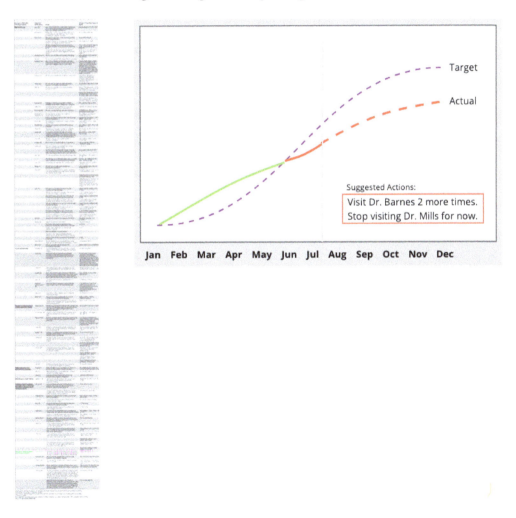

Figure 3: Tabular data on the left and an actionable graph on the right.

This image illustrates the difference between a long list of tabular data (rows and columns of numbers) similar to the data the sales rep received each month and a simple two-line graph that compares the target objective and the actual performance that is dipping below the target. It also includes a suggested action to improve the performance ("Visit Dr. Barnes 2 more times. Stop visiting Dr. Mills for now.").

Practice Observing People

Learning which details to capture during observations comes with practice. A good practice technique is to sit and watch someone doing their job; try to understand what they are doing and possibly why they are doing it. For example, watch people using a directory or information kiosk at a shopping mall. Watch several people to uncover insights you missed with previous observations.

Another good place to practice observing is to go to a store that offers many versions of the same products, like an electronics store, and observe people as they compare similar products. Repeat this several times to uncover user tasks, steps, and Task Dimensions.

An Effective Interview Technique

Typical interviews often include questions about what the users like and don't like about a product. Other ineffective questions include asking which features someone wants or what the product is missing. These questions are unlikely to help you find the root causes of a problem.

Common but poor questions include:

- **Questions about how to improve the design or "what should be changed?"** While this is a common type of question, it often results in inaccurate insights. This question typically results in answers that are based on the current solution. It assumes the current design is close enough to the optimal solution, which is rarely accurate. At best, you are only likely to get suggestions for incremental improvements.

- **Leading questions with inherent biases**, such as "What part of the design do you like most?" What if they don't like any of it, but picked something to be able to answer your question? Leading questions assume something unknown about the user, or try to push the user into a certain frame of mind.

  - "We worked hard on this. What do you think of it?" is leading because we primed people to care about our effort, which makes them more likely to respond in an artificially positive manner.

- **Double-barreled questions ask two questions in one.** "What makes you search for flowers online, and how do you decide to buy?" That sounds like something we want to learn from our research, but we must write questions carefully to ensure that we are asking one question at a time. Asking two questions at once tends to confuse users, and they likely will only answer one of the questions. Focus on one question at a time.

- **Questions that ask people to predict their future decisions.** "Why might you purchase an extended warranty?" is something our marketing and sales departments probably want to know, but is not the right way to ask that question. It would be better to learn more about previous equipment failures. "Have you experienced equipment failures in the past? *Were those failures covered by extended warranties? Why did you buy the warranty? Why didn't you buy the warranty?*"

- **Questions that predict how someone else will react to the product**, such as "How do you think your friends would use this?"

These types of questions evolved out of the old marketing questionnaires of the 1960s and 1970s, but this isn't marketing, and that was fifty-plus years ago. It's time to evolve. A more successful approach is to avoid talking about the product and instead talk about the task. Better questions to ask include questions around:

- **What triggers their task.** The problem or motivation. How do they know they need to do or start something? What happens that causes them to perform this task?

- **Their desired outcome.** What would make them consider this task "completed," and how do people know they are successful? How do people know when they are done?

- **How they approach and solve the problem.** This is the task flow itself, the steps, details, tools, workarounds, and actions the user tries, successfully or unsuccessfully. What's the first thing people do? This might be different things for different people. We want to understand and analyze all possible paths and approaches.

- **Difficulties and pain points.** Where is this task inefficient, frustrating, confusing, difficult, error prone, etc.? We wouldn't ask this directly, but questions like, "What parts of the task are the most difficult to perform?" or "How can this be improved?" can teach us what's a negative user experience. Users know what they find frustrating, confusing, disappointing, or distracting: Debbie Levitt's "Four Horsemen of Bad UX®."

  o "What should be changed?" implies that we only want to know how something that is already there could be altered. It sounds similar to, "How could this be improved?" but this question wording can open up broader and sometimes more imaginative answers.

- One of Debbie Levitt's participants answered, "How could this be improved" by inventing an entire AI-based product that would proactively keep her from impulse shopping. Even though we wouldn't run and build any particular participant's idea, it was very interesting. They might not have come up with that if Debbie had asked a question that sounded like she only wanted to know what in the current interface should be changed.

These types of questions provide more actionable insights than any like/dislike discussion. This interview approach takes practice, but eventually it becomes almost second nature.

Note: explicitly asking questions about pain points often yields inaccurate or incorrect answers. You wouldn't ask a participant, "What is your pain point?" These are just examples of the *types* of questions that lead to valuable insights. You might find another way to get them to describe difficulties and inefficiencies in their processes. Every project, situation, and user is different, and the researcher will need to adjust the question based on these factors.

"If you are only or mostly hearing positive things, you asked the wrong users, the wrong questions, or both."—Debbie Levitt

When "Better" UX Research Questions Are Still Bad

There are various articles and videos trying to teach you how to write "better" research questions. Debbie Levitt reviewed some, and noticed that many of the supposedly better questions were poor, such as:

- **"What are you missing on this website?"** We will know what's missing if we do an observational study and task analysis. We will see how people complete this task now, and what they add to the task to try to improve it. Observing this is always better than asking people what they want or what is missing from an interface.

- **"Which paid features do you use on similar websites?"** Is it important that the feature is paid? And does the user understand which features were paid? Perhaps their job provides this system, and the user isn't thinking about paid or non-paid features at all.

- **"How can you use 'Favorites'?"** and **"How often have you used 'Favorites' on other websites?"** This assumes that something someone does in one system will be done in all systems. Your user might favorite several items on Amazon, and never favorite anything on your ecommerce website.

○ This question also assumes that the frequency of doing something is significant.

○ If we did want to pursue a question like this, we might learn *how many* or *how often*, but did we learn why someone might or might not favorite an item? Do they return to their favorites list?

○ Questions about frequency are often not important to our qualitative studies. The answers might also be found in analytics and other quantitative data, which might be more reliable than people's memories or self-reporting.

○ If exact frequency is not important for the research goals, then these questions should not be asked. Sometimes, "I use it pretty often" is good enough to decide what we're asking next. We might not need the exact number of times per week or month.

- **"In your opinion, how does this feature work?"** One common mistake in observational and evaluative research is to draw the participant's attention to a certain element, feature, or area, and ask them what they think, how they would use it, how it works, etc.

○ It's possible that the user did not see it; this is good information. This isn't a sign that you should draw attention to the element, point it out, and lead people there. Noticing someone *not* using something might be an important observation; either they didn't see the feature or they saw it but didn't think it was applicable. This would be something to ask about in the post-observation interview.

○ If you want to know how (or if) someone will use a feature or how they think it works, write a task that might or might not drive the person to use the feature. But don't write a task that purposefully drives them to the element or feature, such as, "How would you add this to your Favorites?" The answer might be pretty darn obvious, especially if you have a button or icon marked "Favorites."

○ We recommend against directing someone's attention to an element and asking how they think it works. This often (accidentally) validates this feature because the researcher will report that yes, the users knew that "Favorites" saved these items to a wish list or other list. But does that mean the feature worked well? Matched users' needs or tasks? Was intuitive? Was something they would use? Was something they would easily have found themselves?

- **"Explain what you see on the page/screen."** Don't draw people's attention to an element, feature, or screen, and ask them what they see. They will look more closely at everything than they naturally would. This often leads to false validations like, "The user noticed the menu and understood what it would do."

Okay, but does the information architecture and interaction design of the menu work for our users? Does it match their mental models? Does it improve task completion? Did the menu slow people down?

- We don't learn much by asking people to describe what they see on the screen. We should remove these questions. Observing them will show us what they saw, what they missed, and how they used things.

- "Thinking aloud" is a useful method to gain insight into what the user is thinking as they perform a task, but this is different from asking questions about what they see on the screen. Asking what they see distracts them from the more overarching process of performing a task.

- **"Where do you search for the needed information?"** This question is a possibility *only* if the participant already said that they would search. If they have not mentioned searching, then you shouldn't ask where or how they search. That would be leading as you are implying that they search when maybe they don't. You can always ask, "What would you do next?" and keep it open.

- **"Why do you need to undo things?"** Debbie Levitt calls these types of questions "cat's urinary tract" questions. It comes from a 1990s American television commercial for a cat food that helped cats avoid urinary infections. The cat's owner looks right into the camera and says, "Is a cat's urinary tract health important?" There is only one answer to that question, and it's "yes."

  - Undoing is something common we all do often for a variety of reasons. Being able to undo actions is also great for accessibility. Asking *why* someone needs to undo something is likely to only lead to answers we already know. Plus, it sounds like we already know that we need an undo feature or option, so let's invest in accessibility, and just build it.

- **"What do you feel when [site feature] doesn't work?"** Asking about feelings might make us think we will then have empathy, but this is *cat's urinary tract*. When something isn't working, feelings will be negative. Does it matter which feeling users have? Would we design differently if the participant said "frustrated" versus "disappointed" versus "angry"? Let's fix the thing that isn't working.

Capturing Research Insights

Once the observations and interviews are complete, the research team must share their insights with designers, and often with other stakeholders. A common method is to create a formal report, but this is typically unnecessary for the researchers and designers, and possibly even the stakeholders. Few people ever read formal reports, and there are more research phases and tasks to complete before we can work on a final report.

Writing a formal report tends to take a long time and interrupts the research analysis cadence and flow. I have seen teams take weeks to write a report when they could have moved on to conducting task analysis. Moreover, task analysis tends to raise questions that potentially require additional observations or interviews, altering the findings in the report, thus making the report inaccurate/incomplete and not very useful.

At this stage of the research process, rather than a formally written report, creating a list of findings is typically enough to move forward with the analysis. This list will evolve as more analyses and research are completed. At the very least, the list should contain an indication of the task, which user group or type relates to the finding, and what the finding is.

Every project is different, and every list is different. Sometimes it's helpful to include the number of times the finding was observed, the impact of that finding (such as annoyance, error, or task interruption), or the time it took to complete the task. Avoid statements like "75% of users experienced…" when only four users were observed.

What researchers uncover in the observations and interviews are discussed in brief informal discussions. This is an opportunity to share observation insights across the team, especially when different researchers observe different users. At this point, there is no specific way to share these insights such as creating a report. You will only have time to discuss them in a brief conversation. These discussions are mostly intended to suggest what things the researchers should look for in subsequent observations and encourage some consistency across the observations.

Given that this process focuses on task analysis, when observing users, it is important to capture the typical steps they follow to complete their tasks. Focus on the more strategic or cognitive aspects of the task rather than the solution or technology they use. The goal is to describe the task from a solution-agnostic perspective as much as possible; you do not need to capture every button they click.

For example, if someone is using a drawing application, focus more on the tasks they are trying to complete, such as creating an outline of their drawing, sketching the main parts of the drawing, and then trying different colors. It's not important to capture the specific clicks they make in the drawing app.

Trying to capture all of the details in the first observations can inadvertently draw attention to things that are unimportant—"going down the rabbit hole," as the saying goes. Start by simply trying to understand and capture the main steps in the first couple of observations, rather than all of the detail. Focus on capturing the general task steps and artifacts, and note any issues or questions. Specific details are captured with subsequent user observations.

Determining what level of detail to capture in the observations takes practice, so don't worry if you capture too much or too little in the initial observations. Just remember to capture the task flow rather than all the details about the tools the users use. More content about task analysis and task flows will follow shortly.

Getting Buy-In and Improving Collaboration

Throughout the book, these "Getting More Buy-In" boxes contain tips to get small incremental buy-ins rather than a large leap-of-faith at the end when stakeholders first see the final result. Somewhere along this path the stakeholders will have that "aha!" moment where they finally understand how this approach is so much more successful than the typical mediocre UX performed by the competitors.

An inherent benefit of this knowledge-oriented design process is that it lends itself to guiding other people through its evolution. The knowledge-oriented design process generates connected artifacts that actually influence subsequent steps of the process. Rather than making things that you won't use such as journey maps and personas, this process generates artifacts that are linked together from beginning to end.

Once the team knows how to create knowledge-oriented solutions, the next step is to get the rest of the company to buy into this new and novel process. Most people are somewhat habituated to typical UX processes, or assume UX practitioners are there just to approve ideas and sketch screens.

How do we get them to improve their perspectives? This connected relationship of steps and associated artifacts makes it easier to guide stakeholders through the process and promote collaboration. Include stakeholders and other company team members by asking for their feedback along the process *from the different perspectives of each of their roles.* We are not asking them if they agree with the task analysis or "like" or approve of designs. This is collaboration: getting and using feedback at your discretion, not work by committee where you merely get change orders from everyone else. Although you are sharing your work and asking others for feedback, you control the narrative and can apply or disregard any input from the others.

Finding more ways to connect with our teammates creates more concurrence at each stage, which promotes a thorough understanding of how the product ends up with such a novel solution. This avoids the shock of a unique and innovative end result by helping them understand the decision-making journey that drove the design.

One of the advantages of sharing UX artifacts in this manner is that it demonstrates just how much work and knowledge is necessary to perform good UX practices. This can be contrasted against the promise of "Design Thinking," which strips away the important UX expertise and tasks that drive truly successful designs. Well conducted UX research is much more than fake research, rapid brainstorming workshops, and pretty UIs. We must leverage these opportunities to illustrate the value of great UX work.

Sharing the Wealth (of Knowledge)

One way to keep all of the process information in everyone's minds so that they stay connected with the evolution of the design is to create a collaborative community space, a shared physical or virtual wall, some place where everyone passes by regularly, such as a coffee or break room, where you can post representative artifacts generated during the course of the project and process.

Post some of the user knowledge profiles (described later) and the tasks they are associated with, and it won't be long before those profile names develop a life of their own and everyone in the company refers to those profiles by their names. "What would Birthday Bob decide to do in this step?"

Create a space where anyone in the company can post questions on sticky notes. Let them know that you are looking for questions and insights more than critiques of your work. You won't always be able to share all of your artifacts, just some representative ones. Since people will be asking questions, be sure to return and answer some of those questions. Keep it simple and only answer the questions you can. This lets everyone know that their insights are being taken into consideration.

Not only does this keep everyone informed of the progress, it gives them a chance to contribute feedback or questions from their different perspectives, which increases engagement and helps educate folks on the process, encouraging buy-in of the approach. Folks will also begin to understand the difference between UX and UI design.

It helps to use colored dots with numbers on them to connect the strategy, knowledge design artifact, or task step to a wireframe. Place a numbered dot on the item of interest and then place the corresponding numbered dot on the wireframe. This helps people see how the research directly influences the design. Some designers use string to draw lines from an artifact, such as a task flow sticky note, to the wireframe page. Very colorful, but it can get very busy on a complex product design. Nonetheless, it's an easy way to start sharing.

There really is no "done state" for this except when you get to the stage of creating clickable prototypes in (Axure, Figma, Sketch, etc.). You won't be able to put those on the wall easily. This is mostly just an active status board with opportunity for collaboration from others. You don't need to wait for the feedback from the rest of the company if you need to move quickly. This collaboration typically starts off a bit slow and picks up over time. Eventually it becomes part of the company culture.

Case Study: Sharing the Knowledge—Medical Device Design

While working on a medical device design project, we were given the main conference rooms as our collaborative community space to design a new type of device for a startup. The walls were covered in task flows, user knowledge profiles, and design wireframes.

One morning, the CEO said that the company was having an emergency board meeting and he asked if we could take all of the stuff down in the next 5 minutes. We started to, but the Board of Directors started walking in and we had to stop. Apparently, the Board was there to discuss shutting the company down.

About an hour later, the CEO came out and thanked us profusely. It seems the Directors were curious what all of the artifacts on the walls were. The CEO had seen the evolution of our work, and explained the design approach, telling the story of our research and design insights. This impressed the Board of Directors enough that they extended their support and the company became a huge success, selling a year later for almost a billion dollars. The design that resulted from the artifacts displayed on the conference room walls is still regarded as one of the most user-friendly medical devices.

Getting More Buy-In for User Research

Be ready to describe how the current products or design approaches, both yours and the competitors', are missing the point. They are not focused on the users' problems.

Describe the observed problems the users are trying to solve as problems your company can help solve. Avoid talking about the product or design at this point, and focus on the users' problems. Introduce a little bit of the knowledge design opportunities, such as, "We saw that users need a little help with this part of their process."

Keep the discussions at a higher, more strategic level rather than focusing on what the trendiest button colors are, etc. Talk about the users' problems from their perspective. This is too early in the process to have enough concrete data to form a decision or create a design. Give the stakeholders just enough to make them interested in learning more, create anticipation for the next artifacts.

Share some of the high-level findings on the shared wall and allow people to ask questions and submit comments (without proposing solutions). At this point, the goal is to highlight the problems that the users are trying to solve, not how they use any particular solution to solve them. Sometimes, the team members need a gentle reminder that this is the problem identification stage, not the solution or design stage. It's quite common for people to describe things in terms of a solution rather than a problem.

Chapter 4:   Common Research Mistakes

Many teams and individuals conduct research, but it's usually the wrong type of research, which can lead to inappropriate decisions that influence incorrect design approaches. Armed with the arrogance of "we know what our customers need or want," many teams deliberately avoid user research in favor of their own opinions. These opinions are guesses and assumptions that persist, often until a large amount of time and money has been poured into releasing the wrong design into the market. Then we wonder what we got wrong.

For example, the Juicero juicer failed after the designers made (incorrect) guesses about their users.

The Juicero Story

Juicero was a 2016 startup that had received $120 million in funding from famous investors including Google Ventures and Kleiner Perkins. By 2017, they went out of business.

It was a Wi-Fi-connected device that would deliver "fresh" fruit and vegetable juices. You are probably imagining a machine that takes fresh, raw fruits and vegetables, squeeze or grinds them, and turns that into juice. Inexplicably, this $699 USD machine only accepted proprietary packets of juice. To ensure that you only used Juicero packets, the machine had to be connected to the internet to verify the QR code on the packet. Juicero basically took overpriced bags of juice and poured them into your cup.

Or you could buy a container of juice and pour it yourself.

Juicero was a solution in search of a problem, and likely the result of someone who said, "What if we made a coffee pod type of machine, but for fruit and vegetable juice?"

Like the Juicero, many products are the result of brainstorming, ideating, solutioning, or sketching sessions that generate lots of "cool" ideas but don't solve the real problem. These are "solutions looking for a problem to solve," and often lack a correct, well-defined problem statement or a clear UX strategy. Debbie Levitt often calls them a "guess sandwich": we start with guesses and assumptions about our users, and then we add layers of solution ideas, which are also guesses.

Some teammates can become so attached to these designs that they end up justifying them by focusing on the design's benefits rather than critically asking if they solved any of the users' original problems or inefficiencies. A common statement that tries to justify a bad design is "Well, it's better than what we have now," which is a low standard.

When Research Is Skipped or Done Incorrectly

User research is frequently skimped on or skipped altogether in favor of internal assumptions, opinions, or guessing. This should be documented as a project and/or product risk. Minimizing research might satisfy desires to be "fast" and "cheap," but the market is littered with the rotting remains of products and companies who prioritized *speed over quality*.

Without good user research, even good design teams end up solving the wrong problems very well. When we are solving the wrong problem, either well or poorly, there are two possible outcomes: learn that the project is going in the wrong direction during the UX process, or, more often, learn it after the product or service goes live to the public.

"If you don't know where you are going, any road will get you there."
—Lewis Carroll

An accurate solution requires an accurate problem definition. Stakeholders, cross-functional teammates, and even UX practitioners might *think* they know what problem needs to be solved. Taking the phrase, "Let's validate our hypotheses," quite literally, teams conduct cursory research aimed at "validating" and "justifying" the features they already know they want to build. They might skip user research altogether, assuming there is no risk in relying on what they already believe about users and their contexts, needs, mental models, and problems.

Some of the least useful yet most common research mistakes are:

- Conducting research with the wrong users.

- Conducting evaluative research on the existing design during the generative research phase.

- Asking the wrong questions.

- A/B testing to incrementally redesign.

These and suggestions for research methods that gain better results will be discussed later.

Research practices suggested by stakeholders who are not part of the user research effort can undermine the research as well. For example, key stakeholders might significantly change the research stimulus after the research sessions are underway, which introduces inconsistencies in the data and negatively affects the integrity of the research. This is why it is imperative that researchers must control the research and avoid being directed by people who are not trained in or do not understand the complexity of user research.

Research Doesn't Have to Answer a Predefined Question

Many teams believe that research must start with a hypothesis, and then go through a process to prove or disprove it. They mention "The Scientific Method" as the source, but forget that step *three* of The Scientific Method is forming a hypothesis. Step 1 is the generative research that helped identify the hypothesis.

> Observational research is not intended to prove or disprove a hypothesis. It is intended solely to gain objective insights.

When a team or stakeholder has a horse in the race or wants to see their idea built, they "hypothesize" that this idea is the right solution. They often want to skip generative research and assume the hypothesis can't be proven or disproven until a product or feature is released into the market.

A difference between an idea and a hypothesis is how they are phrased. An idea is typically a statement, "our users want to rent a couch in someone's home," whereas a hypothesis is typically posed as a question, "do our users want to rent a couch in someone's home?" Both assume that renting a couch in someone's home is the unmet need, but may miss the true need, that people might just need an inexpensive place close to work where they can take a quick nap.

A hypothesis creates biases that push perceptions into the proverbial "box," both before and after any research is done.

- A hypothesis often focuses researchers on proving or disproving something rather than remaining open to the insights uncovered in the research.

- Focusing on a hypothesis biases the planning, recruiting, methodology, and execution of the research.

- Hypotheses can also bias our research analysis and conclusions, pushing some people to inaccurately classify observations into preconceived groups or conclusions based on the hypothesis.

   o For example, if the hypothesis is that "travelers need a better way to find flights on multiple airlines," then research might focus on finding flights following the typical aggregator models used by all of the travel sites. This research isn't solution-agnostic because we have a hypothesis that we want to focus on, prove, or disprove.

Research should be planned and observations should be made without any preconceived notions or pre-decided solutions. **Simply discover, learn, and understand things without the need to prove or disprove anything in particular.** Be open to what insights the observations uncover. We refer to this early research as generative, discovery, or exploratory research because it generates knowledge or discovers and explores the users' environment to identify unmet needs rather than evaluating the accuracy of a hypothesis.

As mentioned, defining the hypothesis is step three of the Scientific Method:

- Step 1: research and observe.

- Step 2: frame the problem or come up with a question.

- Step 3: create the hypothesis that might answer the question or solve the problem.

- Step 4: design and conduct the experiment that would prove or disprove your hypothesis.

- Step 5: analyze test data and draw conclusions.

This determines whether or not a new solution relies on small changes to an existing solution or needs a complete rethink. We can then go back to step 3 to change the solution so that it better solves the problem from step 2. You cycle around until you have the best execution of the best solution concept.

Sophocles is quoted as having said, "Look and you will find it—what is unsought will go undetected." Whether or not he actually said that, it's the perfect point; having a hypothesis shapes what we will look for and how we will look for it. We might not see what we are not looking for. We might also, consciously or accidentally, drive the research or the findings towards validating the hypothesis, which is flawed research that moves the project, product, and company in wrong directions. In essence, it is not solution-agnostic. The key to good research and discovering unmet needs is "seeing" the invisible.

Asking Users to Solve Their Own Problems

Some research methods attempt to identify and understand users' needs by asking them to describe the problems they have or the solutions they would prefer. We might ask people what's missing from the product, what they want the product to do, and what features they would like to see added to the product. All of these assume that the user understands their own problem well and objectively, and can come up with their own best solutions.

Additionally, people know that something was frustrating, hard to use, or confusing, but they might not know exactly what or why. They are therefore unlikely to know what would make it better. They might guess and create workarounds to overcome limitations or problems with a process or system, but they rarely know the best ways that a product could be architected to truly solve their problems. Consequently, these findings or suggestions tend to be described in relation to the existing solutions and are evolutionary and incremental, not revolutionary.

Some users confidently describe their problem in terms of a solution or a missing feature, which can lead the team to confidently build that feature. But did we truly understand users' problems, and provide the best solution? The age-old quote attributed to Henry Ford (though he never actually said it) exemplifies this well. The quote relating to building the first cars is, "If I had asked my customers what they wanted, they would have said faster horses." With hindsight, we can see that one or more "faster horses" wouldn't replace what a car is and does.

Key problems that arise when users suggest solutions include:

- Assuming the user understands their problem well enough to imagine or design a solution for it. Typically, they don't.

- Users are unintentionally constrained by their own perceptions of what is feasible or possible. They tend to think "inside the box" based on their own experiences with other solutions.

- Focusing on potential solutions decreases the chances of uncovering the root cause of the problem. It's easy to be distracted by discussing ideas and solutions instead of details around pain points and inefficiencies.

- Assuming that researchers or the team can reverse engineer the correct problem definition from the solutions users suggested. This often causes researchers to identify the symptoms rather than root causes.

- The solution the users envision or describe might not be the best solution for themselves or for the majority of your target audience.

- Building "what people said they wanted" typically surprises the team later when users complain or don't adopt the feature.

Irrigation Control

Observations and interviews for an irrigation controller product (turning sprinklers on and off automatically) indicated that users typically don't change the watering schedules for parks and playing fields very much. When there is a special event, rather than changing the irrigation schedule, they might just turn the watering off to avoid interrupting the event with automatic sprinklers. Turning off the sprinklers runs the risk of damaging the grass, but is much easier and less error-prone than changing the schedules, which is a very laborious task that has to be done separately for each field.

If they change the irrigation schedule just for the event, they have to reprogram the normal schedule back into all of the controllers again after the event is over. Also note that controllers can only hold one watering program and have no saved memory of previous programs.

Many users suggested easier programming or the ability to save multiple programs so they can switch between stored programs as possible improvements. What the users really needed was the ability to control the sprinklers remotely. This solves the narrow problem they imagine they have, and provides the solution they need. But what if there's a better way?

Perhaps the irrigation system could remember multiple programs, including ones for special event days. And if remote connectivity is possible, we could allow the users to change or switch between multiple programs from their computer, removing the need to visit an irrigation control panel at every field.

Limitations of Self-Reporting Methods

Methods such as diary studies or asking people to remember and describe their process suffer from inherent self-reporting biases that adversely affect generative research.

Surveys, focus groups, and individual interviews are popular research methods. Despite the well-known fact that what users say is very different from what they actually do, teams often rely on surveys because they are fast and cheap. Teams might prefer focus groups or interviews because they are relatively easy. Anybody can ask users good or bad questions, and mistakenly check "research" off the to-do list. This approach trades expediency for accuracy, and the resulting designs show it. It is far better to prioritize *quality over speed*.

Asking users what they think their problems are often results in inaccurate or incomplete problem definitions. Users tend to only report things that they still see as a problem. They may have created a partial solution for a difficult step of the task. Users commonly create shortcuts, workarounds, cheat sheets, and tricks to fix or improve their processes. When asking them to self-report their problems or process, they might not mention the workaround. In their minds, they have solved the problem. The workaround is now "natural" to them, and they don't see it as a problem any longer, and don't think to mention it when self-reporting their processes or tasks.

Imagine someone explaining a product, but not mentioning how they taped or glued something because a part kept breaking off. That's an important piece of information that we might not learn because it has become a habit or faded into the background of the users' minds.

Debbie Levitt and I conducted an observational study where people were given a task: you have $1,000 to purchase 125 widgets. Nearly everybody grabbed a physical calculator or opened their smartphone's calculator app to find that they had $8 per widget to spend. Here we learned that people wanted to know the price per item, and that they added a step to the task to get that information. If we asked someone the steps they took to research, select, and buy 125 of these widgets, they might not remember to mention "And then I take out a calculator to check my per-item budget."

Researchers must learn what these workarounds are to see where the process had friction points or problems that customers deemed important enough to fix themselves. This is best done by observing people performing the task, and noting the tools, workarounds, duct tape, tricks, cheat sheets, notes, checklists, and other ways they invented to improve the task flow or ensure their success.

Other versions of self-reporting that can end up as flawed research include:

- **"Day in the Life Journal" or diary study.** Asking users to write down everything they do during their day or within the performance of a task seems like a good idea, but is fraught with peril. What users do and say they do are two different things. It becomes tedious to write everything down, so users tend to group some tasks or steps together while leaving others out entirely.

  - This method also relies on the accuracy of their memory since few participants are fastidious enough to truly diary and detail everything they are doing while doing it. They are often reflecting later on what they did, and remembering what they can, or what stands out most to them, which suggests that they will forget to mention at least some of the task.

- **Focus groups** are more commonly used by marketing than by UX, but are still worth discussing. Focus group moderators elicit discussions about a topic or product, but this is a double-edged sword. While it can get people talking, there are many drawbacks, including:

  - **Groupthink.** People prefer consensus and might not speak up when their ideas or opinions seem to run against what others in the room have described.

  - **Fear of judgment.** Sometimes people are not honest or forthcoming on the assumption that others in the group are judging them.

  - **Dominant voice.** One very strong personality in the room can sway the conversation or make more introverted or shy people stay quiet. Sometimes this pseudo leader works to convince others of their opinion, which flaws the results.

  - **Bad questions.** Common questions asked in marketing focus groups are often poor questions when applied to UX research. We shouldn't ask people how much they like a concept (especially if they can't try it right now), how they might use it in the future (they can't predict that), or how their colleagues might use it (they *really* can't predict that). We shouldn't ask people sales questions like would they pay for this, or would they pay (more) for this if we added a particular future feature (another future prediction).

- **Interviews.** Asking users to describe their work, goals, and processes invites the previously-mentioned self-reporting biases. Additionally, users will often neglect to mention something they fear is due to their own ignorance. They're not great at recognizing design flaws, and assume they are "at fault" or lack intelligence. They resist appearing unintelligent to themselves or the interviewer, so they might not point problems out.

- o   When a person is asked how easy something was to use, they are likely to rate or declare it as *easy to use* even if they struggled with it or completely failed the task.

- **Surveys** are so limited in their usefulness in generative UX research and so rarely the right research choice that they deserve a closer focus.

Limitations of Surveys in Generative Research

Surveys seem like a fast, cheap, and easy way to get a number of potential or current customers to share their opinions and preferences. However, surveys are such a poor method for gaining UX insights that successful UX researchers rarely use them for generative research. Here are some problems with designing, executing, or interpreting surveys:

- **Self-reporting biases.** What people claim they prefer or predict they would do usually doesn't match reality. People sometimes want to self-report a better, different, or aspirational ideal rather than reality. Consider those little lies you've told your doctor about how healthy your diet is despite how often you eat fast food.

- **Dishonesty.** Whether it's survey fatigue or the participant hoping to mess with the study, there is always the possibility that the answers do not reflect participants' truths. Consider how many times you've answered a survey question with fake contact information like Mickey@Disney.com or me@me.com, or how often you threw in any answer just to move on.

- **Focusing on quantitative data**. Survey results are often reported as X% of people chose this, or Y% of people want this. However, the heart of UX research is the *qualitative*. We want to know what people do, how they do it, why they do it, and other things that will have color, nuance, variation, and humanity.

  - o   Some teammates believe that the open answers in surveys are good qualitative data, but they are limited data. Actionable qualitative insights come from observing the users and asking follow-up questions.

- **Interpretation of questions and answers**. How often have you selected a survey answer that wasn't really your answer because none of the provided answers matched your reality? How often have you felt unsure of which answer to select because you weren't sure what the questions or answers really meant? Participants struggle with these same things as well.

- **Scales and question types**. Questions are sometimes poorly written, leaving participants feeling like there is no correct answer to the question, or there are multiple correct answers to the question. Debbie Levitt received a survey asking her to rate 10 things in order of their importance to her. Only one was important to her and the other nine were completely unimportant, but ranking all 10 was mandatory. Researchers might incorrectly believe that Debbie's top five ranked items are important to her, but they are not. She only cares about number 1 on the list, and there was no way to communicate that in the survey.

- **Memory.** Some survey questions assume that respondents remember certain things they thought or did in the past. Not everybody has a great memory, and not everybody accurately remembers what they did, how they did it, or why they did it.

- **Leading questions**. The phrasing of questions can bias the answer, often in the direction the researcher desires. For example, "How much do you like Feature X?" immediately biases the response towards liking something to some degree. What if they truly hated it?

- **Meaningless questions** that won't affect the designs. "Do you shop from a desktop computer or phone?" Ultimately, the product has to work on both, and the server analytics will indicate how often different devices or screen sizes are used.

- **The bias of who took the time to fill out the survey**. If the sampling of survey participants doesn't accurately reflect the potential or current customers you were hoping for, the survey is then biased to those who chose to respond. For example, sometimes angrier customers fill out surveys or leave app ratings. This isn't an accurate sample across the target customer base, and may disproportionately reflect the angry users' perceptions.

- **The bias of those who were screened in or out**. Similarly, unreasonably rejecting certain types of participants limits the study. Debbie Levitt often visits Walt Disney World in Florida and has also bought into Disney's timeshare system. The first survey question is Disney's post-vacation survey is, "Where do you live?" Debbie answers (truthfully), "Italy," and the survey is always immediately over.

  o Demographically, Disney parks in the USA don't receive many visitors from Italy, so someone may have decided that those living in Italy are an audience they didn't care about.

  o However, what if the survey had screened for factors other than current place of residence? What if it had screened for how often someone visits the park, if they are part of the timeshare system, or some other element that would help Disney decide who they want to listen to and who they don't? Which part of the customer base do you not want to connect with? Shouldn't outliers be heard?

- o If Italians start visiting Walt Disney World more, Disney is unprepared for them. For example, park maps are available in English, French, German, Spanish, Portuguese, and Japanese, but not in Italian.

- **Manipulated data**. Researchers sometimes manipulate results to push findings in a particular direction. For example, if participants had to rate satisfaction on a scale from 1 through 5, researchers might combine scores of 4 and 5 to show a larger percentage of "happy" people. But why muddy the granularity of a 5-point scale? There might be a good reason to call out people who selected a rating of 4 versus 5.

One positive use of a survey is that it can highlight what the team doesn't know. They might know how many but not who, what, where, when, why, or how. They lack the information to build a proper problem statement. If used well, surveys can open up a conversation about what we don't know, what we are assuming, and our unanswered questions.

Surveys can unfortunately often be wastes of time that lead a project in the wrong direction. Many surveys yield unreliable results, usually self-fulfilling prophecies designed to say what you want to hear. This is often demonstrated in the conflict between marketing, who said people will love this and pay for it, and UX, who learned that people didn't love this and are unlikely to pay for it. Who is right? If that product gets built and launched, a lot of time and money will answer that, and it could be bad news.

Do You Use Onomigo?

In early 2023, Debbie Levitt's company, Delta CX, worked on a generative research study and prepared a screener survey. Debbie had heard about increasing problems where scammers and bots fill surveys out with believable answers, with the intent to fool the system, be included in the study, and receive the financial incentive for participation.

The screener survey asked which websites or apps people use related to their finances. Among the brand names and types of finance apps, Debbie tricked some trickers by including "Onomigo" as a possible financial website or app. Onomigo is a word she made up by misspelling a friend's last name.

Approximately 10% of responses indicated that they use the Onomigo website or smart phone app; neither exist. Disqualifying these respondents helped ensure that the study participants were less likely to be liars or scammers.

But what about the surveys that your company runs? Do you have something in there that would help filter out likely bots and lies? Sometimes a survey will ask the same question twice to see if people answer it the same way, but someone dedicated to their scam might take the time to give consistent—though potentially false—answers for the reward they might get for taking the survey or being included in a larger study.

The Onomigo experiment reminds us that false data may constitute a noticeable percentage of our responses. There might be more false responses than our margin of error, which brings our confidence in this data into question.

Although we can't always catch every bot and scammer, consider including a completely made-up choice somewhere in your survey so that you can filter out or quarantine people who select that answer.

Card Sorting in Research

The three methods of card sorting (closed, open, hybrid) involve allowing participants to organize elements into meaningful groups. While not an explicit self-reporting mechanism, card sorting does rely on the user's interpretation of the cards and they organize them based on those perceptions, which is an implicit self-reporting effect. The "cards" inherently bias the users by virtue of the terms used on them. Users tend to focus their thinking along the lines of those terms. If given 30 cards with different terms for desserts, users are likely to focus their thinking on only desserts.

- One common application of card sorting is to create software menu structures or information architecture, but this can also have issues. When given a list of terms, users often mistakenly believe that a card can be in one and only one group. One approach to overcome this is to provide multiples of the cards, but that might be more confusing, especially if the card sorting system requires participants to use every card.

- Card sorting is more useful for identifying information architecture elements than it is as a generative research tool.

"It's Good Enough"

Sometimes it takes great lengths to get alignment with teammates or stakeholders. One Air Force project involved redesigning a rescue radio for downed pilots. The radio was designed without using observational research, and a subsequent UX design audit demonstrated that the radio was very difficult to use.

The engineering and development team balked at the notion that their design was hard to use, so one of the stakeholders took a bunch of the engineers into the desert without much water. After they were delirious from the heat, they were given one of the rescue radios and told to call for help. Only then did the team understand the frustration a downed pilot in the middle of the desert experiences as they fumbled with the awkward interface of the radio.

Sometimes it takes a bit of work for the team to have that "aha!" moment. Hopefully, it won't take dropping the team in the desert without water to make a point or get alignment.

Confident internal tech teams who understand the product very well, are tech savvy, and do not often use the products in the same way end users do typically fail to appreciate the nuances of design that make the difference between a functionally accurate design from a truly usable one. Techies declare, "It works for me!" and the assumption is that if the Engineering Lead can use it, so can the fighter pilot in the desert. So can Grandma. So can people with disabilities and accessibility needs.

They can slap each other on the back and declare that the product is "good enough" and ship it. But when the feedback comes in and users are struggling, complaining, or failing, who will be held accountable? What will it cost the company to diagnose the failures and fix them?

Common Observation Errors

Observational research has its difficulties as well. Inexperienced researchers tend to make the same common observational mistakes. You likely have committed some of these mistakes as well, knowingly or unknowingly. Learning what the mistakes are helps us avoid them in the future.

- **Observing current designs.** As mentioned earlier, researchers observing users interacting with the current design may mistakenly assume that the existing design solves the right problems. However, this assumption is nearly always incorrect. Observe users trying to solve their problem without focusing on any one solution. This is referred to as being solution-agnostic.

    o Observing the existing product design results in little more than an audit of the current design, and fails to identify truly innovative insights. User actions are typically limited to what the tools provide and are typically an inaccurate representation of how the users want to or could perform the task.

    o Observing various solution approaches may not be optimal, but it will at least expose the researchers to different ways the users try to perform their task and provide a broader perspective.

- **Time and motion studies.** Without proper guidance, many researchers make the mistake of merely recording users' actions and behaviors without understanding *why* users were doing those things. These simple "time and motion" studies can result in incremental improvements, such as reducing the amount of time it takes to complete a task. However, if you're looking for disruption or innovation, these studies are unlikely to uncover ground-breaking unmet needs. They tend to just identify where to reduce the time on task, not what the root cause of the users' problems are.

- **Automating current frustrations.** Many teams identify observations that focus on refining the current design, which typically involves investing effort towards automating the user's current tasks rather than redefining the problem. The current design forces the users to follow a specific process. Adding automation to current solutions doesn't necessarily solve root problems.

- **Interrupting the user.** The act of observing changes the observation. Researchers might not be familiar enough with the domain to understand everything they are observing and interrupt the user to ask about an observed event. This interruption, however brief, disrupts the user's cognitive processing and can change them from a performer to a teacher, thus altering their subsequent behavior.

    o   It is far better to note questions and ask the user in a post-observation interview. You might also have a SME participating in the observations who can field your questions without interrupting the user.

- **Observing only part of the complete task sequence.** Consider a popular model of a kitchen blender. It looks great and you love to use it, but you hate to clean it. The top has all kinds of nooks and crevices that are difficult to reach with a sponge or brush. The dishwasher doesn't clean it thoroughly unless it's positioned in a precise orientation. Cleaning is part of the task flow, but it is obvious that the cleaning tasks were not part of the design consideration. The design could easily include design features that improve the cleaning and maintenance tasks.

Most products fail to serve the complete user task, leaving gaps in the task sequence. Companies commit large budgets to promote brand loyalty, encouraging repeat purchases within the brand. Failing to attend to the full arc of the product experience can jeopardize that loyalty, and increase business risk.

Who Should Conduct UX Research?

Non-UX researchers around the organization probably have not trained in UX research processes. They may not be good at recognizing and avoiding their natural biases. They might create flawed research from bias in planning, recruiting, and questions to bias in analysis, synthesis, and recommendations.

Graphic designers, web developers, product managers, project managers, business analysts, engineers, stakeholders, and marketers may have their own forms of research for their specific roles and purposes, but these do not replace UX research. UX researchers are trained in cognitive and behavioral sciences, leading them to plan and execute research differently.

UX research done by trained specialists will lead to more and better insights than other roles doing their own research or "trying their hand" at UX research. Trained researchers know what to look for and how to avoid mistakes that interrupt or invalidate the observations.

Market research is typically focused on getting user perceptions or reactions to concepts or products; this is not the same as UX research. Asking a user what they think they might do or like in the future typically yields inaccurate answers.

For example, Walmart conducted research asking their customers, *"Would you like Walmart aisles to be less cluttered?"* What did they think the customers would say? Might customers want the aisles to be *more* cluttered? It's a *cat's urinary tract* question. Nonetheless, Walmart spent 5 years and hundreds of millions of dollars to "unclutter" their aisles. The result? They lost $1.8Bn in sales. ["Walmart Declutters Aisles per Customers' Request, Then Loses $1.85 Billion in Sales," April 18, 2011, https://consumerist.com/2011/04/18/walmart-declutters-aisles-per-customer-request-then-loses-185-billion-in-sales/]

What happened here? Non-UX researchers applied their common form of research, a reaction-oriented survey, rather than a UX-focused research method to identify user behaviors. Doing the wrong research is just as bad, if not worse, than doing no research. The wrong research gives false confidence in the "findings," and typically leads teams to justify the wrong design approaches. We check off the research box as done, and we move forward with what we think we know. If no research is done, it opens the door for questioning.

PART 3: TASK ANALYSIS AND USER KNOWLEDGE PROFILES

Chapter 5: Task Analysis

Now that you have conducted some initial user research, learn how the users' observed task processes can be transformed from notes to task flows. We'll also examine how researchers can mitigate the business risk mentioned in the previous section.

Task analysis is a practice introduced in Don Norman's Cognitive Science curriculum. I studied under Don at the University of California, San Diego, from 1988-1990. I evolved task analysis over time by adding tips and tricks learned from other HCD practitioners, plus my experience on over 250 projects. There is no perfect or single way to do this. Every project is different, and this process can be adjusted. The basic process is fundamentally successful, but feel free to experiment with it, adjusting it to fit your needs.

The objective is to capture each of the steps of the users' task in an ordinal manner, identifying the artifacts or issues related to each step of the task. This version maps the task step vertically, starting at the top and flowing downwards with artifacts and issues captured to the side of the associated step. The process works regardless of your visual style; you are welcome to try other styles of mapping or diagramming to see if they work better for you.

A task analysis is not a single-pass event. It may take several passes to complete a complex task flow. A simple task flow can take days; an extremely complex task or set of tasks can take weeks to accurately diagram. The first pass should capture the high-level aspects and major steps of the task. In a second round of analysis, each of these major steps can be further analyzed, leading to the creation of additional task flows. Sometimes the team may need to analyze these flows a third time to create yet another level of task specificity or precision.

It helps to identify which user type (described as a user knowledge profile later in the book) is performing each task flow. Avoid combining different profiles' task flows. It's better to separate the flows so that each one addresses the needs of a single user knowledge profile. This will be demonstrated shortly.

After capturing the task details, a critical step in this process involves optimizing the task flows to identify opportunities to make the system do more of the work for the users and eliminate friction points.

Four Phases of Task Analysis and User Knowledge Profiles

A task analysis is a series of four increasingly precise phases that include defining users' perspectives relative to the tasks they are trying to complete. Each phase focuses a little deeper on the details of each of the tasks.

- **Phase 1: The Big Picture.** Understand the major steps of the task domain.

- **Phase 2: Second Pass.** Understand the task flows in more detail, updating user definitions with new insights.

- **Phase 3: User Knowledge Profiles.** Identify and define the different user types for the various tasks based on their knowledge profiles.

- **Phase 4: Optimize the Task Flow.** Redefine and optimize the task flows.

Phase 1: The Big Picture

Task analysis comes from properly planned, conducted, and analyzed generative observational research. Don't guess or assume what the users' tasks or steps are.

Using the research notes, create a flow diagram of the major elements of the main tasks, roughly four to eight major steps for each key task. Any more than that is not a big-picture perspective.

The typical task analysis identifies these elements:

- **Trigger.** The problem, question, or event that motivates the user to perform the task. This is why they started the task.

- **Desired outcome.** What it takes to solve their problem, answer their question, or complete the task. This is what they want as the result of performing the task.

- **Task flow.** The steps of the task from trigger to desired outcome. This represents how they can step through the task.

Map these at a high level for each task and user definition. Don't worry about being too precise. There is no single perfect way to do this; the point is to capture the essence of the tasks.

Task Analysis Practice: Buying Flowers

Using our earlier example of buying flowers, start with the trigger and the desired outcome to identify the scope of this task.

- **Trigger:** forgot wife's birthday.

- **Desired outcome:** please wife so she accepts the apology.

In between these, some sort of magic will happen that will take our user from their unfortunate trigger to their desired outcome. For your first pass, fill in the gaps with a few main steps. Further details will come out in the next pass.

- **Trigger:** realize that they forgot the occasion.

- Determine that flowers are the right gift.

- Enter the flower shop.

- Review flowers.

- Select flowers.

- Purchase flowers.

- Wife receives flowers.

Note: when observing users buying flowers in a flower shop, the team paid special attention to observing users who needed to have their flowers delivered rather than carrying them out of the store with them. The delivery tasks observed in-store were similar to the types of tasks that users would perform online.

Our task analysis technique uses different colors of sticky notes to denote specific aspects of the flow. Note that these colors are arbitrary and simply reflect the colors that were available in the common five-color packs of sticky notes. You can use any colors available to you; just be consistent, and consider colorblind-friendly colors.

- **User actions on green sticky notes.** Things the user does. These are the steps of the task; they might be manual or cognitive.

- **System actions on yellow sticky notes.** Things the system must do. The "system" might be technology or anything other than the user. It's something that could be seen as a task step, but the step is not performed by the user.

- **Artifacts on purple sticky notes.** Tools, knowledge, workarounds, hints, and anything used in a particular task step, whether or not the artifacts improved the user's task success.

- **Questions or issues on orange sticky notes.** Problems, blockers, or questions around a particular task step. These often need to be investigated with further research or addressed in the optimized task flow.

- **Miscellaneous on pink sticky notes.** Used for everything else, such as titles, triggers, desired outcomes, etc.

- We also borrow a diamond shape from logical flowcharting to show decision points and where a user has options or possible paths.

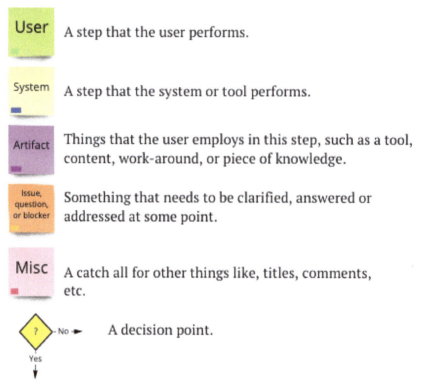

A step that the user performs.

A step that the system or tool performs.

Things that the user employs in this step, such as a tool, content, work-around, or piece of knowledge.

Something that needs to be clarified, answered or addressed at some point.

A catch all for other things like, titles, comments, etc.

A decision point.

Figure 4: This is a visual legend of the five sticky note colors. In order, top to bottom, they are User (green), System (yellow), Issue (orange), Artifact (purple), Misc (pink) and a decision point (a yellow diamond with "Yes" and "No" arrows leading off of it). We used Miro for the examples in this book, and we added Miro "tags" to each note. That way, the note says what type it is. Even if someone can't perceive the colors, they can still see if it's User, System, Issue, Artifact, or Misc.

A task flow diagram might follow this pattern:

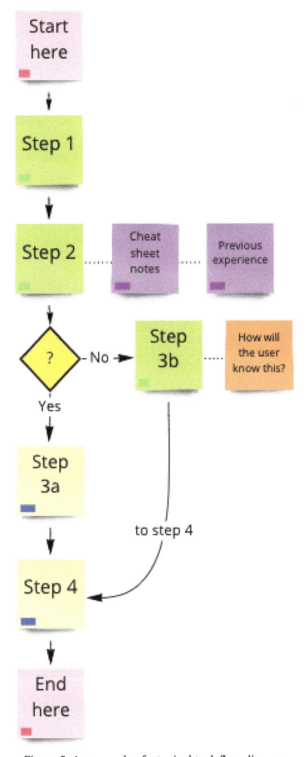

Figure 5: An example of a typical task flow diagram

The above task analysis image shows the following flow:

- **Misc:** Start here.

- **User:** Step 1.

- **User:** Step 2. **Artifacts:** Cheat sheet notes, previous experience.

- **Decision:** Yes: go to Step 3a. No: go to Step 3b.

- **User:** Step 3b: Goes to Step 4. **Issue:** How will the user know this?

- **System:** Step 3a (if previous decision was "yes").

- **System:** Step 4.

- **Misc:** End here.

As mentioned before, user steps and actions tend to be diagrammed vertically, flowing downward. The artifacts, issues, and miscellaneous notes are aligned horizontally next to their associated actions. Sometimes an issue might also be represented as an artifact, and vice versa. Again, this is not a perfect or precise process; just capture the essence of the task.

ProFlowers Task Flow, First Pass

Here's how the main steps of the ProFlowers example might look for the first pass:

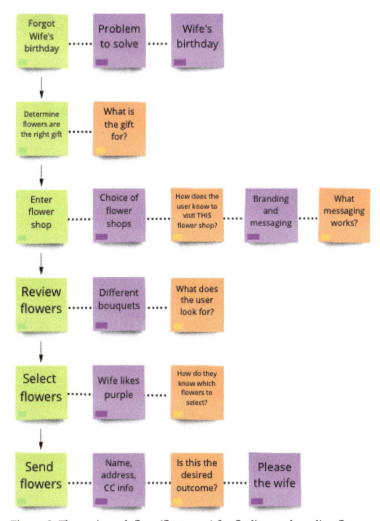

Figure 6: The main task flow (first pass) for finding and sending flowers.

Figure 7: Legend of the sticky note colors: User (green), System (yellow), Issue (orange), Artifact (purple), Misc (pink).

ProFlowers Task Flow, First Pass:

- **User:** Forgot wife's birthday. **Artifact:** Problem to solve, wife's birthday.

- **User:** Determine flowers are the right gift. **Issue:** What is the gift for?

- **User:** Enter flower shop. **Artifact:** Choice of flower shops. **Issue:** How does the user know to visit *this* flower shop? **Artifact:** Branding and messaging. **Issue:** What messaging works?

- **User:** Review flowers. **Artifact:** Different bouquets. **Issue:** What does the user look for?

- **User:** Select flowers. **Artifact:** Wife likes purple. **Issue:** How do they know which flowers to select?

- **User:** Send flowers. **Artifact:** Name, address, credit card info. **Issue:** Is this the desired outcome? **Artifact:** Please wife.

Phase 2: Second Pass

It's time for the second pass at our task analysis diagram. Take each of the user (green) or system (yellow) sticky notes from the first pass of task analysis, and identify the more detailed steps that accomplish that part of the task. Provide enough detail to capture the sequence of events or decisions that occur through the task flow. This will include adding user actions, systems actions, artifacts, issues, etc.

One way to accomplish this is to think about how each main user or system action can be broken down into smaller, more detailed steps. The purpose is to represent the tasks well enough to redefine the tasks and optimize them later. Determining the amount of detail appropriate for each project comes with practice. The right level of detail would include all of the main steps a user must take to complete a task, but does not need to include minor steps such as error or confirmation messages.

The second pass of the ProFlowers example analysis illustrates what this might look like. Again, it doesn't have to be perfect, just representative. Keep in mind, this will be replaced by the optimized version later.

ProFlowers Task Flow, Second Pass

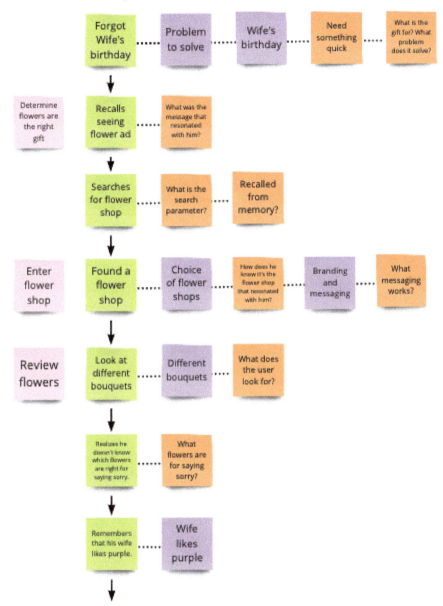

Figure 8: Part 1 of the second pass of the ProFlowers task flow.

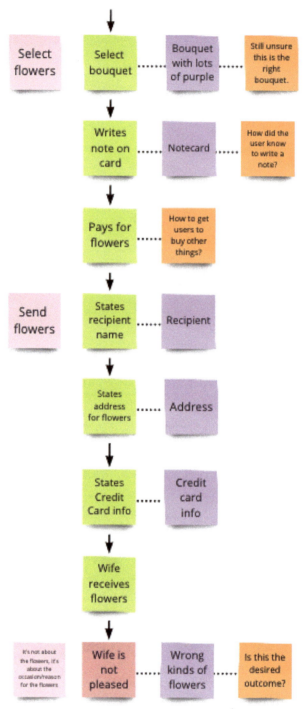

Figure 9: Part 2 of the second pass of the ProFlowers task flow, continued from part 1. These are split up only because of the limitations of a printed book. Your diagram would not be broken into parts.

Figure 10: Legend of the sticky note colors: User (green), System (yellow), Issue (orange), Artifact (purple), Misc (pink).

ProFlowers Task Flow, Second Pass:

- **User:** Forgot wife's birthday. **Artifact:** Problem to solve, wife's birthday. **Issue:** Need something quick. What is the gift for? What problem does it solve?

- **Misc:** Determine flowers are the right gift. **User:** Recalls seeing flowers ad. **Issue:** What was the message that resonated with him?

- **User:** Searches for flower shop. **Issue:** What is the search parameter? Recalled from memory?

- **Misc:** Enter flower shop. **User:** Found a flower shop. **Artifact:** Choice of flower shops. **Issue:** How does he know it's the flower shop that resonated with him? **Artifact:** Branding and messaging. **Issue:** What messaging works?

- **Misc:** Review flowers. **User:** Look at different bouquets. **Artifact:** Different bouquets. **Issue:** What does the user look for?

- **User:** Realizes he doesn't know which flowers are right for saying sorry. **Issue:** What flowers are for saying sorry?

- **User:** Remembers that his wife likes purple. **Artifact:** Wife likes purple.

- **Misc:** Select flowers. **User:** Select bouquet. **Artifact:** Bouquet with lots of purple. **Issue:** Still unsure this is the right bouquet.

- **User:** Writes note on card. **Artifact:** Note card. **Issue:** How did the user know to write a note?

- **User:** Pays for flowers. **Issue:** How to get user to buy other things?

- **Misc:** Send flowers. **User:** States recipient's name. **Artifact:** Recipient.

- **User:** States address for flowers. **Artifact:** Address.

- **User:** State credit card info. **Artifact:** Credit card info.

- **User:** Wife receives flowers.

- **Misc:** It's not about the flowers, it's about the occasion/reason for the flowers, Wife is not pleased. **Artifact:** Wrong kind of flowers. **Issue:** Is this the desired outcome?

Capture the Knowledge Requirements

One of the key elements of creating the user knowledge profile in the next phase is identifying the knowledge requirements of the task. This includes identifying the common knowledge that a typical user would have, as well as the knowledge the users will need (but won't likely have) in order to achieve the task.

During the observation, think about the observed user knowledge, how someone knows to do something. Consider how the user comes to gain or have that knowledge. Is that knowledge a common knowledge element of that domain? For example, nurses are trained and familiar with the many procedures for administering medications: shots, pills, ointments, etc. That is common domain knowledge that every nurse could reasonably be expected to have. A key objective for nurses is to avoid dangerous drug interactions. Given the tens of thousands of possible drug interaction combinations, there is no reasonable expectation that the average nurse will know them all.

This is an example of knowledge required to achieve their objective. The difference between knowing how to administer medications and which interactions to avoid identifies a knowledge gap.

The common mistake in conducting an analysis of the users' process flow is to create a flow diagram of how the users use the current solution, website, service, or tool (think journey map), rather than focusing on the actual task, independent of a solution (solution-agnostic). Researchers make elaborate diagrams of how people are expected to use the existing product or design without investigating how users actually want or need to perform their tasks.

This tends to highlight how people use the product more than identifying the requirements of the task process, leading to incremental improvements of the current solution rather than revolutions in the domain.

Focusing on the current design misses the knowledge requirements of the task and typically only identifies the requirements of using the current design. So be sure you are analyzing the knowledge requirements of the task and not just the current design.

Capturing Negative Paths

The first pass of the task flow should capture the main steps to successfully complete the tasks and achieve the desired outcome. The second pass can capture the negative paths, what happens when something goes wrong (user or system error), or at least indicate where a negative path occurs. If it is a simple negative path, such as an invalid credit card error, use a single sticky note to indicate where it occurs. You can revisit these negative paths during the optimization step.

Typically, it's not necessary to capture all of the details of a current negative path; just indicate that they exist. If the negative path remains after creating the new optimized task flow, then you should optimize that remaining negative path task flow, as well.

For example, typical ecommerce websites include shopping carts, which all have potential negative paths, such as items that become "out of stock" because another user buys the last remaining item at the same time as this user adds the item to their cart. If, like in the ProFlowers example, there is no shopping cart, then this negative path would need a different design solution.

Complex Paths

Teams new to task analysis might find very large and complicated diagrams unwieldy. It might be better to map the complex flows as a set of separate flows, which will be explained below. Complex tasks can be captured by creating a series of separate tasks flows that branch off from other sticky notes. Indicate how the sub-tasks are connected, such as labeling the exit point of one flow and the corresponding entry point in another flow with a circle with a letter. A goes to A, B to B, etc.

This allows you to work in bite-sized chunks rather than on the whole task at once.

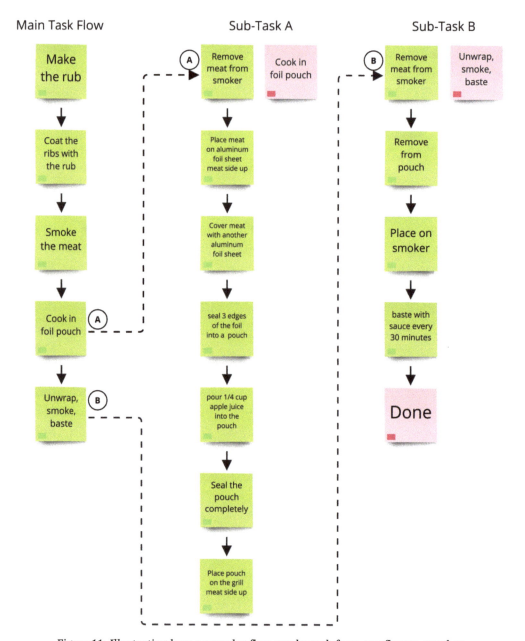

Figure 11: Illustrating how a complex flow can branch from one flow to another.

The general flow for cooking ribs on a smoker grill might go something like this:

- **Main task flow:** Make the rub; coat the ribs with the rub; smoke the meat; cook in foil pouch; unwrap, smoke, baste.

- **Subtask A** branches off from the "cook in pouch" step and shows more detail for that step: Remove meat from smoker; place meat on aluminum foil meat side up; cover meat with another aluminum foil sheet; seal 3 edges of the foil into a pouch;

pour ¼ cup of apple juice into the pouch; seal the pouch completely; place pouch on grill meat side up.

- **Subtask B** branches off from "unwrap, smoke, baste" step to show more detail: Remove meat from smoker; remove from pouch; place on smoker; baste with sauce every 30 minutes; done.

Make separate flows for each of the main steps identified in the first pass. If the first pass included five main steps, then the team could create up to five separate detailed flows in the second pass. Include a pair of lettered circles to indicate where the task flow connects to the next task flow.

Note: In some cases, you may need to do three passes or levels of detail to capture all of the complexity of a large task: a first pass of the main steps, a second pass with a bit more detail, and a third pass with all of the detail.

A common question regarding this process is, "How much detail should the task flow include?" There is no prescriptive formula that defines the level of detail you should include. It depends on the domain and the tasks. You will likely initially analyze these task flows in too much detail, and that's okay. With practice, you will find the right amount of detail for your projects. Keep in mind that these task flows are just an intermediate step to get you to the optimization step; many of these task steps will be changed or eliminated.

Phase 3: User Knowledge Profiles

User Knowledge Profiles Rather Than Personas

Personas, as they are defined and used in common User-Centered Design (UCD) processes, are typically useless artifacts. It's quite common for teams to spend weeks creating personas, only to never use them again. The weakness of the typical persona is that they are too vague and tend to capture meaningless data that does not relate to the product or problem.

For example, how does knowing that a user is a college graduate with two kids and a minivan help you design a kitchen appliance retail site? More generally, how does the typical persona influence the UX strategy or even the UI design? It doesn't.

In his book *About Face*, Alan Cooper described personas differently than I and other UCD experts defined them. We had conversations with Alan Cooper during his research for *About Face*, but something was lost in translation. This knowledge-oriented UX profile description is a better representation for the typical "persona" since it focuses on the user's knowledge of the specific task and task flow, which directly influences the design of the website or product. If personas cannot inform strategies, decisions, or designs, they might be a good-looking artifact, but they are useless and not actionable.

Debbie Levitt frequently reviews UX practitioners' portfolios. She remembers one where the persona was described as having many problems with their online banking and used a Windows laptop. When the practitioner came to the solution and design, it was an app aimed at helping people find online courses. This persona was described as using a laptop and needed help solving her problem. The solution was an app (for a mobile device, not a laptop) that offered online courses, expecting the persona to take the courses and solve their own problem. This is an example of a meaningless persona, unused even by the practitioner who created it.

Here are some key mistakes that can render personas meaningless:

- **Based on demographics**, irrelevant characteristics that incorrectly, inaccurately, or incompletely influence the design. Unless a website or product specifically solves a problem for one demographic, the typical demographic, psychographic, or socio-economic data people like to add to personas are of no value. Common but non-actionable information we often see in personas includes:

    o The user drives a minivan.

    o The user is 70% kind.

    o The user likes the Starbucks® brand.

    o The user is ISFJ according to Myers-Briggs® (MBTI).

- **Personas are not persons.** Most persona descriptions are generic. Rather than describing the characteristics of a specific user in a specific situation, they describe a generic person who is applied to many different situations. Many personas are defined as a role or title, such as Manager or Sales Director. These are job titles and are much too general to influence a design.

- **Aspirational characteristics.** The persona must be based on what was learned during UX research. Do not add traits to personas based on guesses about the customers. Do not assume which tasks they will perform afterwards.

- **Overgeneralizing.** A persona described as "being adept at creating Microsoft Excel® charts" might be considered an expert Excel user. Would that persona still be an expert if the task were to create pivot tables, which they had never done before? Be careful of assigning the users a savviness that they might not have for the given task just because they are savvy in another task.

    o Debbie Levitt once saw a UX practitioner's portfolio where a persona was labeled as "tech savvy," and then was described as needing her husband to help her with everything related to her computer and phone.

- **Guesses and assumptions.** Do not leave persona creation to groups, teams, stakeholders, workshops, or anybody who will either apply their own biases or make guesses and assumptions about customers. Anybody saying, "We don't need to research; we know what people want," should not be present when personas are being created.

Check That the Target Audience Actually Exists

A client once requested that I determine the effectiveness of an existing product they intended to repurpose into the medical domain. The research identified a user knowledge profile that was clearly *not* who the client had expected. The original product relied on people with large and strong hands (likely to be male) to use the device. The actual end users were quite different: they were nursing assistants, many of whom were females with small hands.

Observations clearly identified that this new set of users lacked the strength necessary to use the device correctly. This demanded a complete redesign of the tool to allow smaller and less powerful hands to use it effectively. Simply reusing the original design would have been an expensive failure.

Debbie Levitt once worked on a project where the client declared that their target audience was "promiscuous gay men in San Francisco who want to get tested for sexual diseases, but don't want to tell their doctor about their habits." The client was sure that since these men would be too embarrassed to discuss their private lives, they would avoid using their insurance or healthcare, and want to pay cash for medical lab testing.

Debbie was suspicious of this invented persona for the entire project, and was not surprised when eight well-recruited usability testers volunteered during the moderated study that they would never pay cash for lab tests. They would talk to their doctor and use their health insurance, or go to a free clinic and pay nothing. Debbie later learned that the client had a health insurance company as an investor. One might surmise that the investor wanted to target customers they assumed had reasons to avoid using their health insurance.

Unlike the typical persona, user knowledge profiles are not separate, independent artifacts but are integral components of a task flow. Each user knowledge profile is tied to a specific task because the knowledge related to that task is typically specific to that task. Profiles should be defined by cognitive, behavioral, and knowledge characteristics rather than demographics and psychographics.

Unlike personas, knowledge profiles are so closely related to a particular task that they shouldn't be socialized or shared without their contextual relationship to the task. They are task-specific. You do want to share them, but make sure they are associated with your task analysis.

Rather than creating a generic persona that applies to the entire project, create user descriptions that are specific to a given task. This results in more profiles, but they will each be tied to a single, specific task.

Disabilities and Accessibility Needs

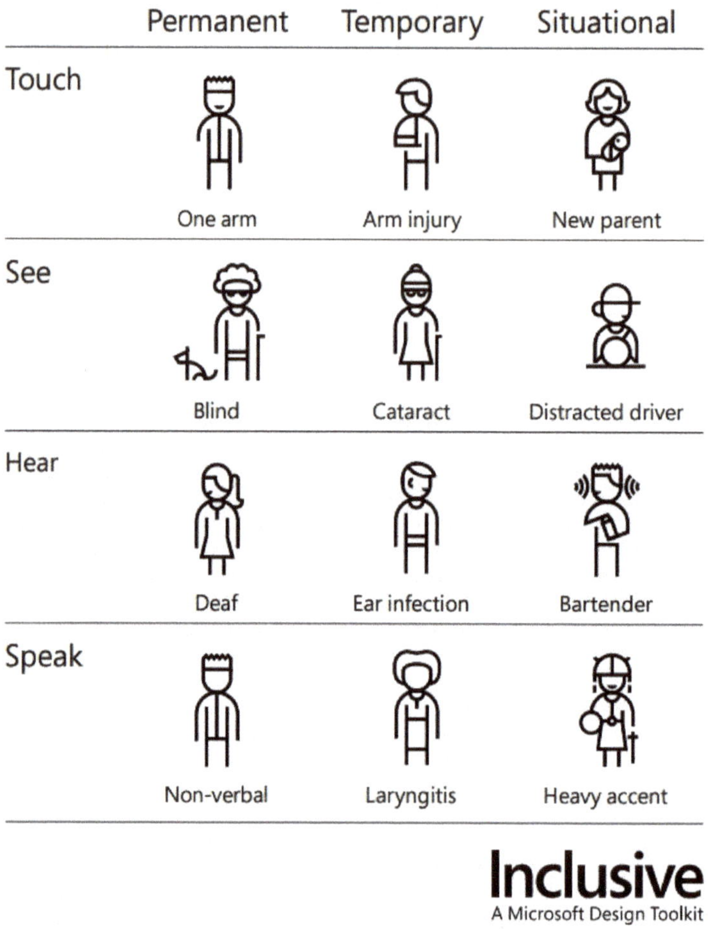

	Permanent	Temporary	Situational
Touch	One arm	Arm injury	New parent
See	Blind	Cataract	Distracted driver
Hear	Deaf	Ear infection	Bartender
Speak	Non-verbal	Laryngitis	Heavy accent

Inclusive
A Microsoft Design Toolkit

Figure 12: Image taken from Microsoft's Inclusive Design Manual. Explained below.

Those with disabilities or accessibility needs must be included too, as many of the disabilities affect user knowledge and cognition when performing the task. Knowledge profiles tend to focus on the cognition and behavioral aspects of the users. Tasks are likely to include seeing and/or hearing, thinking, and motion, even if the motion is inputting responses into the digital interface. Consider the task you are studying, which senses are involved, and how disabilities, diagnoses, or conditions might change how users approach the task.

Microsoft's Inclusive Design model reminds us that disabilities might be permanent, temporary, or situational.

- **Permanent** disability. Deafness is a permanent disability. Wearing a cochlear implant is not a cure. As soon as the user takes off their bionic ear, the world falls silent.

- **Temporary impairment.** The person will interact with the world differently for a limited or short time. Examples include an arm injury or an ear infection. It's a different experience than for someone with a permanent disability.

- **Situational impairment.** External conditions cause someone to change how they consume information or interact with the world. For example, trying to listen to a phone call inside of a noisy restaurant is a situational hearing disability.

Pay particular attention to user disabilities and note anything that can be addressed in the eventual solution that might better fit a range of needs. For example, medical equipment meant for use in patients' hospital rooms were initially designed with various audible alarms to alert care-givers of emergency situations. Given that there were often several devices in the room, nurses didn't readily recognize which device was alarming, even though each device had a different type of alarm. This prompted the designers to add additional visual alerts to help identify which device was alarming.

Frequent and Infrequent Tasks

The design objective is to improve the user's success at performing tasks and achieving their desired outcome. Therefore, it is imperative to understand users from perspectives of **knowledge**. What knowledge can the typical user reasonably be expected to have regarding this task? What knowledge will they need—but won't have—to successfully complete this task?

This is very task specific since the same person will have different knowledge levels or user knowledge profiles for different tasks. It's also important to recognize whether this is a frequent or infrequent task for this user knowledge profile. An infrequent task suggests that the design will require helping the user a little bit so that the task is easy to complete with little knowledge.

Think of a wizard approach as a way to help the user with an infrequent task. The popular American personal income tax software, TurboTax®, provides a quasi-wizard approach that works very well for doing taxes, which is a once-a-year event of a complex, laborious, and unwanted task. Users file their income tax forms once a year to determine if they have paid enough tax throughout the year, owe money, or if they will receive a refund for overpayment. Since they only file once per year and tax laws change every year, users aren't likely to be familiar with how to complete the required tax forms, many of which are rather complex and confusing. These forms require accurate information and calculations, and mistakes, whether intentional or not, can incur significant penalties.

Let's get an idea of your financial picture

Select anything that applied in 2018.

Had a job (W-2)

Donations to charity

Bank account interest (1099-INT)

College expenses/tuition (1098-T)

Paid student loan interest (1098-E)

Received dividends (1099-DIV)

Retirement plan withdrawal (1099-R)

Self-employed (1099-MISC, expenses)

Vehicle registration fees

I sold or traded Cryptocurrency

Show more

It's OK to pick something even if you're not sure if it applies. We'll help you figure that out later.

Figure 13: The TurboTax® start page with selections for different tax questions or situations.

The TurboTax initial screen asks users to select various types of financial activities that might impact their tax situation, such as "Had a Job," "Donations to Charity," and "Bank Account Interest."

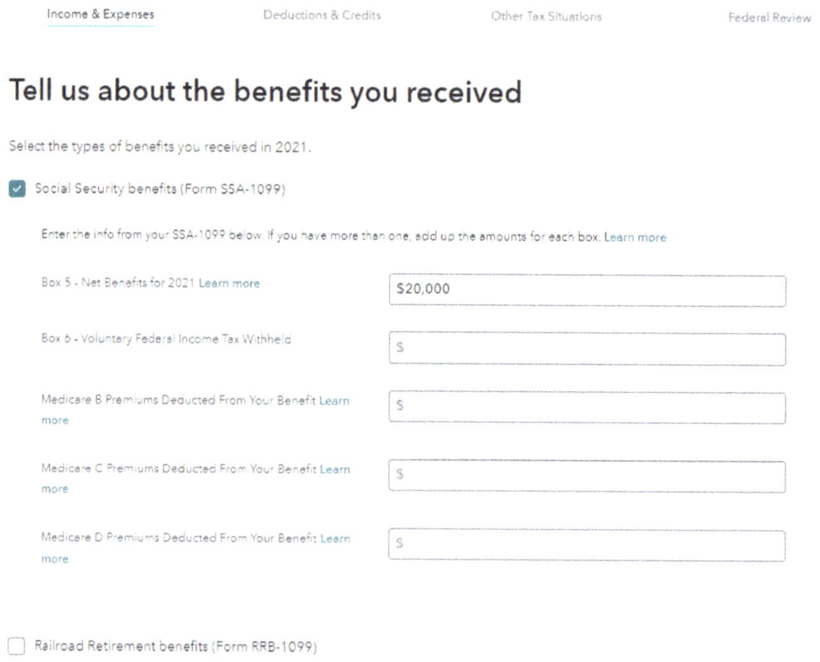

Income & Expenses   Deductions & Credits   Other Tax Situations   Federal Review

Tell us about the benefits you received

Select the types of benefits you received in 2021.

☑ Social Security benefits (Form SSA-1099)

Enter the info from your SSA-1099 below. If you have more than one, add up the amounts for each box. Learn more

Box 5 - Net Benefits for 2021 Learn more
$20,000

Box 6 - Voluntary Federal Income Tax Withheld
$

Medicare B Premiums Deducted From Your Benefit Learn more
$

Medicare C Premiums Deducted From Your Benefit Learn more
$

Medicare D Premiums Deducted From Your Benefit Learn more
$

☐ Railroad Retirement benefits (Form RRB-1099)

Figure 14: An example wizard-style screen from TurboTax.

Users are taken step by step through their tax preparations by answering simple questions, such as whether they got married or sold property this year. They don't even feel like they are doing their taxes!

A frequent task suggests that the design must be easy to use. A common American personal finance software, Quicken, takes a more efficient design approach to their software since users are likely to use it on a more frequent basis and perform the same tasks repeatedly. It's interesting to note that TurboTax and Quicken® were owned by the same company for many years, yet used different design approaches for their two related products with different usage models.

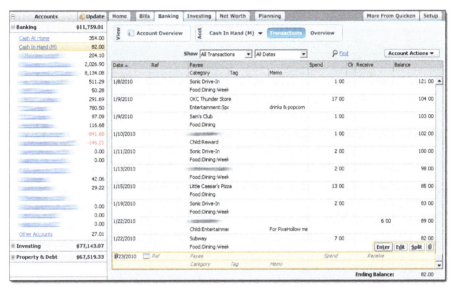

Figure 15: A check register from Quicken. Note the inline editing design. This is more efficient than a wizard approach that would walk a user through writing a check or entering an expense.

Simple interfaces are more appropriate for infrequent or unfamiliar tasks, or tasks that demand zero errors. Interfaces for more frequent tasks *can* be a little more complex, but must still be organized, ordered, and easy to use. The goal for frequent tasks is to enhance expediency and efficiency. In my experience, users tend to find overly simple interfaces cumbersome and laborious for repeated tasks.

Task-Oriented, Knowledge-Based Profiles

Elements that typically make up a task-oriented user knowledge profile include:

- **Objective.** What drives them to want to complete the task? Why are they doing this? This is usually described as an overarching goal.

- **State of mind.** Sometimes it's important to know what the typical state of mind is when performing this task. Are they typically hurried, stressed, confused, interrupted, distracted, etc.? Users' changed or reduced cognitive abilities might influence the design approach.

- **Trigger.** What event or need prompts the task to begin? This can be the specific problem or event that initiates users' actions.

- **Desired outcome.** How does the user know when the task is complete? What is the expected end result? What does that result look like to the user? How will the user know they have achieved their objective? Knowing the answers to these questions helps focus the design towards solving the user's problems in ways that meet or exceed their expectations.

- **Common knowledge base.** Users typically come to a website, product, or service with a common set of knowledge about the problem space. This may include equipment they are familiar with such as phones, tablets, or websites, or it may include specific domain knowledge. It is important to understand what your team or company expects users to know about their task, tools, and environment.

  o Task frequency and domain or technology savviness are important to capture. The more frequently the user performs the task, the more likely they are familiar with it.

  o In cases where there are both infrequent and frequent users of a task, it might be better to create two separate profiles for the same task since you must design for both. This may also include creating two different optimized task flows, one for each user type.

  o Individual knowledge and skill can vary widely, which leads to variability in the user knowledge profile definition. It's acceptable to capture the most common 80% of the users. It's nearly impossible to capture all of the user knowledge profile characteristics in one profile.

- **Required knowledge.** It is even more important to understand what knowledge the user must have—but might not—in order to complete this task successfully. This will likely show up in the task analysis and can be addressed in the optimized task flow. The goal of this entire process is to reduce or eliminate this knowledge requirement.

- **Knowledge gap.** Pay particular attention to the difference between what users are expected to know (common knowledge) plus what they need to know (required knowledge), and what they don't know or understand (knowledge gap). The main objective of knowledge-oriented design is to identify and bridge that knowledge gap.

- **Artifacts.** Take note of the various items that people use in performing their tasks such as notes, guides, checklists, cues, etc. These indicate knowledge elements that users don't have in their heads but need to know to complete the task successfully. These are often indicators of knowledge gaps or assistive objects used to overcome a knowledge gap.

Name:		Trigger:
		Outcome:
		Common K_n:
Objective:		Required K_n:
		K_n Gap:
State of Mind:		Artifacts:

Figure 16: A blank user knowledge profile template. Note: the K_n is a common abbreviation for the word "knowledge."

ProFlowers User Knowledge Profile

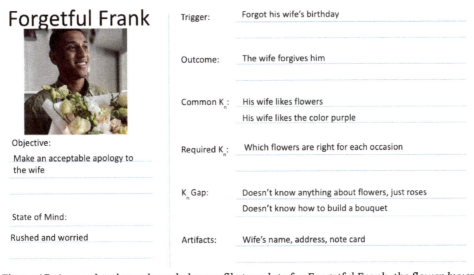

Forgetful Frank	Trigger:	Forgot his wife's birthday
	Outcome:	The wife forgives him
	Common K_n:	His wife likes flowers
		His wife likes the color purple
Objective:	Required K_n:	Which flowers are right for each occasion
Make an acceptable apology to the wife		
	K_n Gap:	Doesn't know anything about flowers, just roses
		Doesn't know how to build a bouquet
State of Mind:	Artifacts:	Wife's name, address, note card
Rushed and worried		

Figure 17: A completed user knowledge profile template for Forgetful Frank, the flower buyer.

- **Name:** Forgetful Frank

- **Objective:** Make an acceptable apology and please his wife.

- **State of mind:** Rushed and worried.

- **Trigger:** Forgot his wife's birthday.

- **Outcome:** Forgiveness from his wife.

- **Common knowledge (K_n):** His wife likes flowers, and she likes purple.

- **Required knowledge (K_n):** Which flowers are right for each occasion.

- **Knowledge (K_n) gap:** He doesn't know anything about flowers, just roses. He doesn't know how to build a bouquet.

- **Artifacts:** Wife's name and address, a note card.

Adding more detail to the task flow identifies additional characteristics of the users related to each specific task. Update the user knowledge profiles throughout the task flow analysis as new information is uncovered. The tasks and profiles will likely evolve as the team analyzes them in more detail.

A Design Strategy Evolves

Uncovering and designing for important aspects of the task that competitors missed can revolutionize a product domain. These unmet needs are the key to truly disruptive designs. If the analysis has not identified a new unmet need, then it's likely that the research or analysis wasn't done well. This takes practice, but it helps to always be looking for the user's knowledge gap. This is typically where an unmet need exists. I call the moment you recognize an unmet need the "aha moment."

At this point in the process, a design strategy begins to evolve. It's not important to design yet. But pay attention to one or more strategic opportunities that the unmet need reveals. This might be a good time to share these strategic insights with key stakeholders to get their input on how the business and marketing aspects (among others) of the product might affect these new unmet needs. Uncovering unmet needs typically opens up new opportunities that might impact how the company markets itself or the product. These are strategic-level decisions that can influence the optimization steps to follow.

For example, imagine researching why your company's marketing and advertising aren't as effective as they could be. The research might show that the product was promoted in a way that actually had little value to the customers. I had a client for whom the research identified an unmet need that required a shift in the company's website design and messaging approach. The task optimization could go in one of two directions: to either support the current marketing plan, or to support a new marketing plan focused on the freshly discovered unmet need. They opted to change their marketing to better address the unmet need and are doing great now with a dramatic increase in customer queries and sales.

Phase 4: Optimize the Task Flow

Identifying the task flow, pain points, hurdles, issues, and artifacts prepares us for the next step: streamlining the task flow, where we envision making the system do more of the work for the user, and eliminating user pain points. Optimizing the task flow occurs after the second pass is complete, when there are no more steps to break down into smaller details or flows.

Repeat: Automation Isn't the Answer

Optimizing the task flow is the opportunity to improve the task, not just the design or UI. A common mistake many designers make is to simply automate the existing task flow. Automating existing designs still relies on the same highly variable user skills and knowledge. Such designs can only succeed at a level no greater than each user's highly variable level of skill and knowledge.

For example, one recent project had a UI that mimicked a spreadsheet that users had created to solve their problem. The spreadsheet had its own inherent limitations, and was essentially a workaround. The automated version included the same limitations without improving the task. They ended up with an app that looked and acted like the spreadsheet without making the system to do any work for the user.

Make the System Do the Work

In our optimized task flow diagram, making the system do more of the work means replacing the green sticky notes (user actions) with yellow sticky notes (system actions). You are removing user actions, streamlining the process, removing negative Task Dimensions, and having the system do more of the work for the user. You are dramatically reducing user efforts, errors, the dependency to complete the task with the existing user knowledge, and you are promoting a best practice approach to performing the task.

A typical indicator that the task is optimized well is that the task flow will look very different from the original task flow, and different from what competitors have created. The optimized task flow will likely seem more efficient, though efficiency isn't always the goal. You might find that you are highlighting an element of the task that no one else is focusing on. If the optimized task flow looks pretty much like the original flow or is similar to what the competitors have created, then consider reviewing the analysis. Something was missed. A well-optimized flow will be very different from the more "manual" flow.

Optimization is not typically a one-to-one switch from a green to a yellow sticky note. Sometimes it's only a partial transition. Sometimes the system will need to perform many actions to replace the green sticky.

For example, the following flows (from the ProFlowers project) are a section of a larger flow, but they illustrate how parts of the task are changed to have the system do things for the user. Some of the changes include doing things the user couldn't do at all or could only do partially:

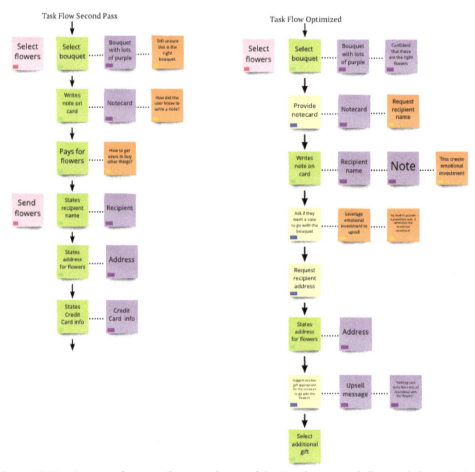

Figure 18: Two images of part or the second pass of the ProFlowers task flow and the optimized task flow illustrate how the existing task flow ("second pass," on the left) shows all green (user) actions, whereas the optimized flow illustrates how half of the tasks can be performed by the system.

Compare the two ProFlowers task flows, the second pass and the optimized version, to see how the task was optimized to get the system to do some of the work for the user. As a result, greens (user actions) were replaced with yellows (system actions), which made the task easier for the user. A more thorough example of the difference between a second pass flow and the optimized flow is provided below.

ProFlowers Task Flow, Second Pass

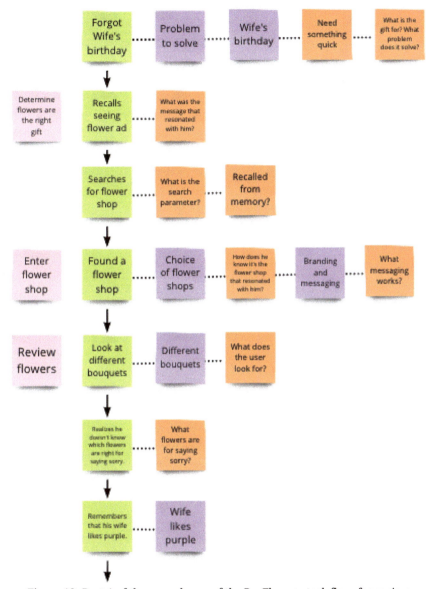

Figure 19: Part 1 of the second pass of the ProFlowers task flow, for review.

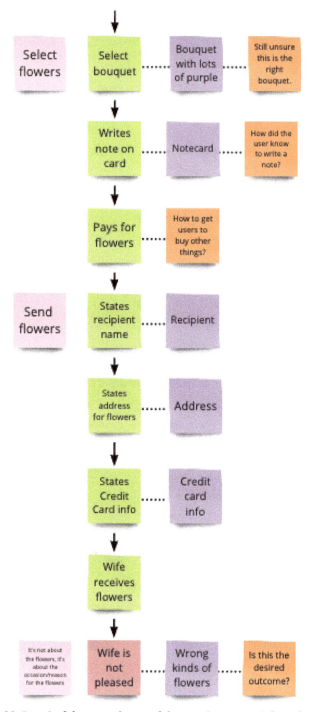

Figure 20: Part 2 of the second pass of the ProFlowers task flow, for review.

ProFlowers Task Flow, Second Pass:

- **User:** Forgot wife's birthday. **Artifact:** Problem to solve, wife's birthday. **Issue:** Need something quick. What is the gift for? What problem does it solve?

- **Misc:** Determine flowers are the right gift. **User:** Recalls seeing flowers ad. **Issue:** What was the message that resonated with him?

- **User:** Searches for flower shop. **Issue:** What is the search parameter? Recalled from memory?

- **Misc:** Enter flower shop. **User:** Found a flower shop. **Artifact:** Choice of flower shops. **Issue:** How does he know it's the flower shop that resonated with him?; **Artifact:** Branding and messaging. **Issue:** What messaging works?

- **Misc:** Review flowers. **User:** Look at different bouquets. **Artifact:** Different bouquets. **Issue:** What does the user look for?

- **User:** Realizes he doesn't know which flowers are right for saying sorry. **Issue:** What flowers are for saying sorry?

- **User:** Remembers that his wife likes purple. **Artifact:** Wife likes purple.

- **Misc:** Select flowers. **User:** Select bouquet. **Artifact:** Bouquet with lots of purple. **Issue:** Still unsure this is the right bouquet.

- **User:** Writes note on card. **Artifact:** Note card. **Issue:** How did the user know to write a note?

- **User:** Pays for flowers. **Issue:** How to get user to buy other things?

- **Misc:** Send flowers. **User:** States recipient's name. **Artifact:** Recipient.

- **User:** States address for flowers. **Artifact:** Address.

- **User:** State credit card info. **Artifact:** Credit card info.

- **User:** Wife receives flowers.

- **Misc:** It's not about the flowers, it's about the occasion/reason for the flowers, Wife is not pleased. **Artifact:** Wrong kind of flowers. **Issue:** Is this the desired outcome?

ProFlowers Task Flow, Optimized

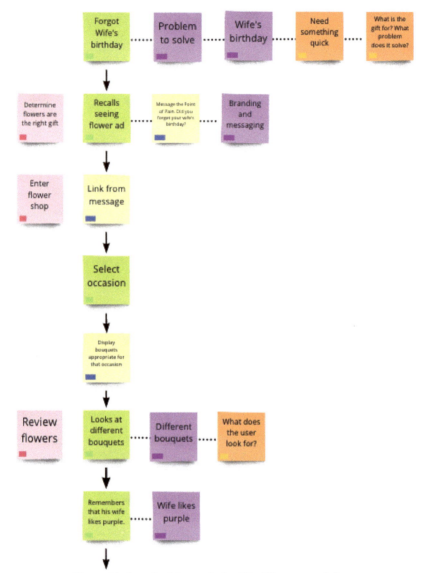

Figure 21: Part 1 of the optimized ProFlowers task flow.

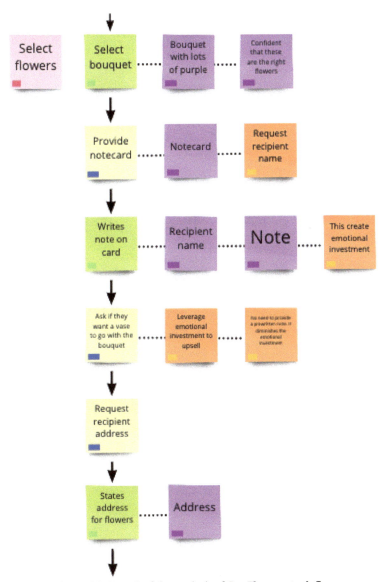

Figure 22: Part 2 of the optimized ProFlowers task flow.

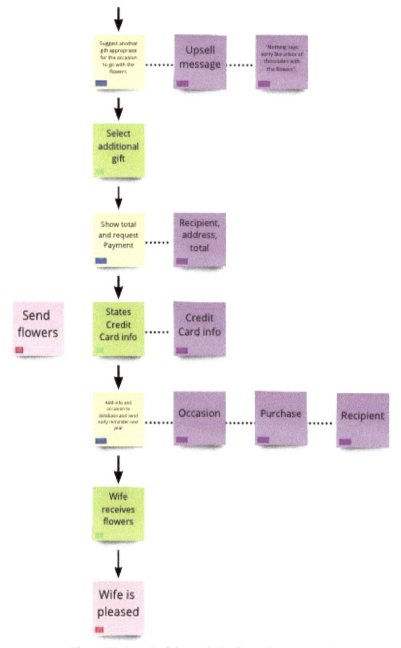

Figure 23: Part 3 of the optimized ProFlowers task flow.

Figure 24: Legend of the sticky note colors: User (green), System (yellow), Issue (orange), Artifact (purple), Misc (pink).

ProFlowers Task Flow, Optimized:

- **User:** Forgot wife's birthday. **Artifact:** Problem to solve, wife's birthday. **Issue:** Need something quick. What is the gift for? What problem does it solve?

- **Misc:** Determine flowers are the right gift. **User:** Recalls seeing flowers ad. **System:** Message the pain point: Did you forget your wife's birthday? **Artifact:** Branding and messaging.

- **User:** Search for flower shop. **Issue:** What is the search parameter? Recalled from memory?

- **Misc:** Enter flower shop. **System:** Link from message.

- **User:** Select occasion.

- **System:** Display bouquets appropriate from that occasion.

- **Misc:** Review flowers. **User:** Look at different bouquets. **Artifact:** Different bouquets. **Issue:** What does the user look for?

- **User:** Remembers that his wife likes purple. **Artifact:** Wife likes purple.

- **Misc:** Select flowers. **User:** Select bouquet. **Artifact:** Bouquet with lots of purple, confident that these are the right flowers.

- **System:** Provide note card. **Artifact:** Note card. **Issue:** request recipient name.

- **User:** Writes note on card. **Artifact:** Recipient name, note. **Issue:** This creates emotional investment.

- **System:** Ask if they want a vase to go with the bouquet (this helps the user who may not think to add a vase). **Issue:** Leverage emotional investment to upsell. No need to provide a prewritten note. It diminishes the emotional investment.

- **System:** Request recipient address.

- **User:** States address for flowers. **Artifact:** Address.

- **System:** Suggest another gift appropriate for the occasion to go with the flowers. **Artifact:** Upsell message, "Nothing says sorry like a box of chocolates with the flowers."

- **User:** Select additional gift.

- **System:** Show total and request payment. **Artifact:** Recipient, address, total.

- **Misc:** Send flowers. **User:** State credit card info. **Artifact:** Credit card info.

- **System:** Add info to database and send early reminder next year. **Artifact:** Occasion, Purchase, Recipient.

- **User:** Wife receives flowers.

- **Misc:** Wife is pleased.

Irrigation Controller Case Study

In the irrigation project mentioned earlier, the client was an average-performing company that had relied on its 30-year-old design approach with declining success. Their commercial irrigation control product was indistinguishable from its competitors, and the client needed to shake things up a bit in order to earn more market share.

Spoiler alert: The resulting solution strategy was very different from the rest, and became the buzz throughout the industry. It was so novel that even though the competitors became aware of this new approach, they lacked the knowledge to solve the new unmet need because they had not done any of this research or task analysis.

Research and Insights

Early observational research clearly indicated that the existing product served only a fraction of the total user task needs. The original product was designed to irrigate on a set schedule, but schedule changes were risky and tedious for the user to handle. Once the schedule was changed, it was just as tedious to revert back to the previous schedule. Consequently, this rescheduling process invited numerous user errors that constantly frustrated the users. These errors include:

- **High cognitive demand.** Keeping track of the programming changes.

- **Manually intensive actions**. Reprogramming the controllers several times.

- **Knowledge dependencies.** Knowing which changes to make.

This issue was common to all of the competitors' products; they all made the same mistake. Based on the research findings, the new strategy changed the design approach to focus on *accommodating frequent schedule changes*, including predictable schedule changes, and the ability to revert back to the standard schedule with ease.

The Problem

Bobby is the Parks and Recreation Manager responsible for all of the playing fields. She has to prepare the county's various baseball fields for the annual end of summer three-day baseball tournament. The normal watering schedule would make the fields unplayable, so she must make several changes leading up to, during, and then after the tournament. This means lots of changes to the irrigation controllers.

Current Task Flow

1. **Identify which fields will be used and when games are scheduled on them.** The schedule is to play three games on each field on Friday, two games on each field on Saturday, and then one game on several fields Sunday, with one field having two games, the second being the championship game.

2. **Overwater each field for two days before the baseball tournament, then water lightly each evening.** This means changing the regular watering schedule from Sunday-Tuesday-Thursday nights, to something more complicated.

3. **Check the fields each day to make sure an error hasn't been made.**

4. **Return to the normal watering schedule after the tournament.**

This task flow requires a lot of sprinkler controller schedule changes and, as past mistakes will attest, errors do occur. The sprinkler controller settings are not easy to change, requiring dozens of interactions for each controller, and a field might have multiple controllers.

Each of the above changes would need to occur at each field. Since each field was constructed at different times, they will have different makes and models of controllers, which increases the potential for user error. Each schedule change involves dozens of clicks or button pushes for a total of hundreds of setting changes on at least three occasions.

Keep in mind that the manager would not be setting the controllers herself. She would entrust that responsibility to the field techs, who are not the most experienced users in this domain. The potential for human error is high.

Irrigation Task Flow, First Pass

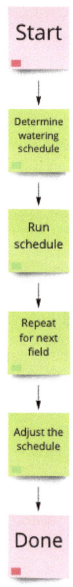

Figure 25: First pass of the irrigation example task flow.

Irrigation Task Flow, First Pass

- **Misc:** Start.

- **User:** Determine watering schedule.

- **User:** Run schedule.

- **User:** Repeat for next field.

- **User:** Adjust the schedule.

- **Misc:** Done.

Irrigation Task Flow, Second Pass

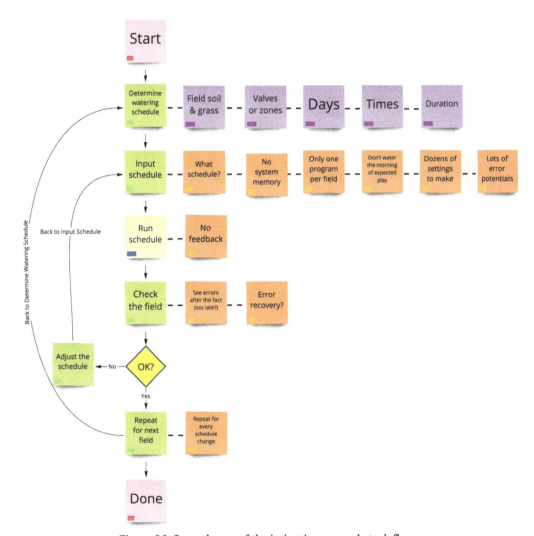

Figure 26: Second pass of the irrigation example task flow.

Irrigation Task Flow, Second Pass:

- **Misc:** Start.

- **User:** Determine watering schedule. **Artifact:** Field soil and grass, Valves or zones, Days, Times, Duration.

- **User:** Input schedule. **Issue:** What schedule? No system memory, Only one program per field, Don't water the morning of expected play, Dozens of settings to make, Lots of error potentials.

- **System:** Run schedule. **Issue:** no feedback.

- **User:** Check the field. **Issue:** See errors after the fact (too late), Error recovery?

- **Decision:** OK? **No:** go to **User:** Adjust the schedule. **Yes:** go to **User:** Repeat for next field.

- **User:** Adjust the schedule, go back to Input schedule.

- **User:** Repeat for next field, go back to Determine watering schedule; **Issue:** Repeat for every schedule change.

- **Misc:** Done.

User Knowledge Profile

The following is an example based on the needs of the parks and recreational fields manager preparing for an annual county-wide three-day baseball tournament.

- **Objective.** Keep the fields in playable condition throughout the tournament.

- **Trigger.** A special event, such as a three-day baseball tournament.

- **Desired outcome.** Prepare the fields and keep them in playable condition all three days despite the heat and increased play they will be subjected to.

- **Common knowledge.** The manager understands the basics of watering grass fields for regular weekend play usage. They will know that watering too much leaves fields vulnerable to damage, but not enough dries them out and damages them as well. They know they are expected to keep water usage to a minimum and to save water where possible.

- **Required knowledge.** The manager will need to know different watering programs to water each field, preparing them for extraordinary usage. For example, how to water the fields ahead of the event to strengthen the grass, but don't water the morning of an event because it leaves the field soft and vulnerable to damage. The goal is a watering schedule that optimizes water usage, keeps the fields playable, and minimizes damage.

- **Artifacts.** An optimized watering schedule.

- **State of mind.** Slightly worried; under pressure to avoid a mistake; unsure of a new irrigation protocol, but motivated to try a new protocol.

Irrigation User Knowledge Profile

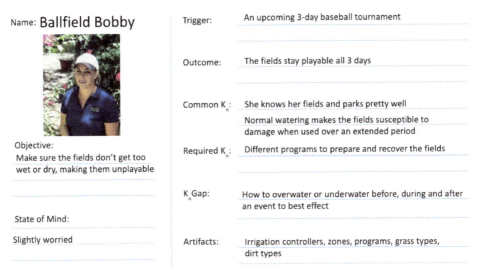

Name: **Ballfield Bobby**

Objective:
Make sure the fields don't get too wet or dry, making them unplayable

State of Mind:

Slightly worried

Trigger: An upcoming 3-day baseball tournament

Outcome: The fields stay playable all 3 days

Common K_n: She knows her fields and parks pretty well

Normal watering makes the fields susceptible to damage when used over an extended period

Required K_n: Different programs to prepare and recover the fields

K_n Gap: How to overwater or underwater before, during and after an event to best effect

Artifacts: Irrigation controllers, zones, programs, grass types, dirt types

Figure 27: The user knowledge profile for the irrigation example.

This is a completed user knowledge profile, including the related information. Note the elements that define the knowledge gap: the difference between what the user knows *and* what they need to know but won't. Required knowledge minus common knowledge is our knowledge gap that we must try to bridge.

- **Knowledge gap.** How to overwater or underwater before, during, and after an event to best effect. The proper watering schedule based on her event, grass type, and soil conditions. A specific watering schedule that optimizes water usage, keeps the fields playable, and avoids damage to the fields, which relies on overwatering and underwatering effectively.

Our later question will be how to provide best practices knowledge to improve the success of this event without relying on the variable skills and knowledge of each user.

Irrigation Task Flow, Optimized

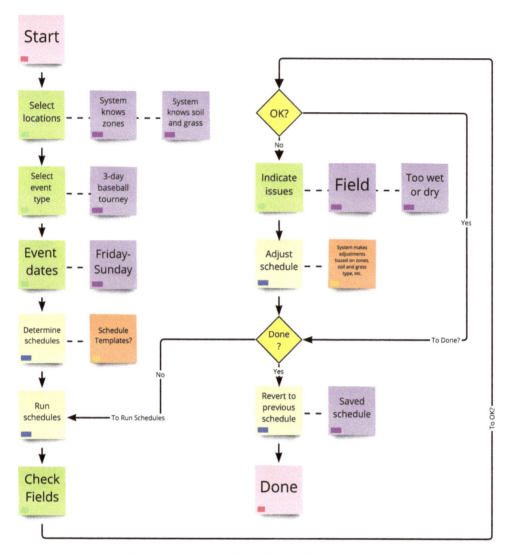

Figure 28: Optimized flow of the irrigation example.

Figure 29: Legend of the sticky note colors: User (green), System (yellow), Issue (orange), Artifact (purple), Misc (pink).

Irrigation Task Flow, Optimized:

- **Misc:** Start.

- **User:** Select locations. **Artifact:** System knows zones, System knows soil and grass.

- **User:** Select event type. **Artifact:** 3-day baseball tournament.

- **User:** Event dates. **Artifact:** Friday-Sunday.

- **System:** Determine schedules. **Issue:** Schedule templates?

- **System:** Run schedules.

- **User:** Check fields.

- **Decision:** OK? **Yes:** Go to **Decision:** Done? **No:** Go to **User:** Indicate issues.

- **User:** Indicate issues. **Artifact:** Field, Too wet or dry.

- **System:** Adjust schedule. **Issue:** System makes adjustments based on zones, soil, and grass type, etc.

- **Decision:** Done? **No:** Go back to **System:** Run Schedules. **Yes:** go to **System**: Revert to previous schedule.

- **System:** Revert to previous schedule. **Artifact:** Saved schedule.

- **Misc:** Done.

User Feedback

Initial user feedback indicated that this new design strategy promised to disrupt the industry and increase the client's market share. The telltale sign was when customers indicated that they were delaying their planned purchases until the new product was ready. When was the last time you heard about a new design disrupting the market *before* being released?

Chapter 6:   Example Project: A Travel Problem

This example project will evolve throughout this book to illustrate the concepts presented in each chapter. The information in this example is derived from an actual project, and is accurate enough to provide real-world practice with these concepts.

Travel Project Scenario

Pat is an executive currently in Los Angeles (LA) for a client event. They just learned that they need to be in New York City (NYC) the next evening for a client dinner. Pat has never been to New York City, and is unsure of where things are and how to get around. The client dinner will be at 7:00 p.m. in midtown Manhattan, and Pat will want to stay in a nearby hotel.

Because of evening commitments in Los Angeles, Pat can't take a red-eye flight (common U.S. slang for an overnight flight). How does Pat figure out their NYC travel plans?

Issues Pat needs to address include:

- How early to leave the hotel in Los Angeles.

- How to get from the hotel to the Los Angeles (LAX) airport.

- Which airport to use in NYC. There are three: EWR (Newark), JFK (Kennedy), and LGA (LaGuardia).

- Which flights have first-class seating available.

- Which flights have Wi-Fi so Pat can research the new client and feel prepared for the dinner meeting.

- The best NYC hotel for Pat's needs. Pat focuses on their preferred hotel brands and airlines to reduce the search effort.

- How to get from the NYC airport to the hotel. Should Pat rent a car in NYC?

Note that this list does not specify which websites were used or how they were used. We have only detailed what Pat is trying to accomplish. We are solution-agnostic, and would observe many people matching Pat's profile as they use various sites and solutions.

Travel Task Flow, First Pass

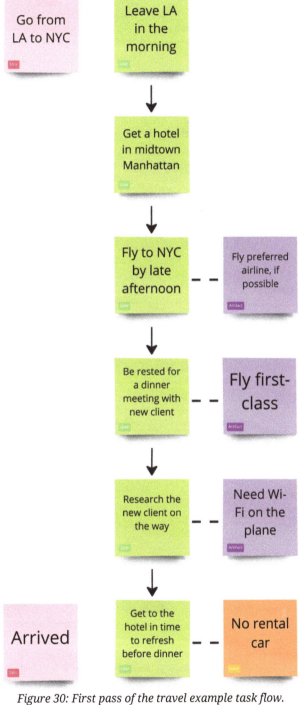

Figure 30: First pass of the travel example task flow.

Travel Task Flow, First Pass:

- **Misc:** Go from LA to NYC. **User:** Leave LA in the morning.

- **User:** Get a hotel in midtown Manhattan.

- **User:** Fly to NYC by late afternoon. **Artifact:** Fly preferred airline, if possible.

- **User:** Be rested for a dinner meeting with new client. **Artifact:** Fly first class.

- **User:** Research the new client on the way. **Artifact:** Need Wi-Fi on the plane.

- **Misc:** Arrived. **User:** Get to the hotel in time to refresh before dinner. **Issue:** No rental car.

Travel: Task Flow Second Pass

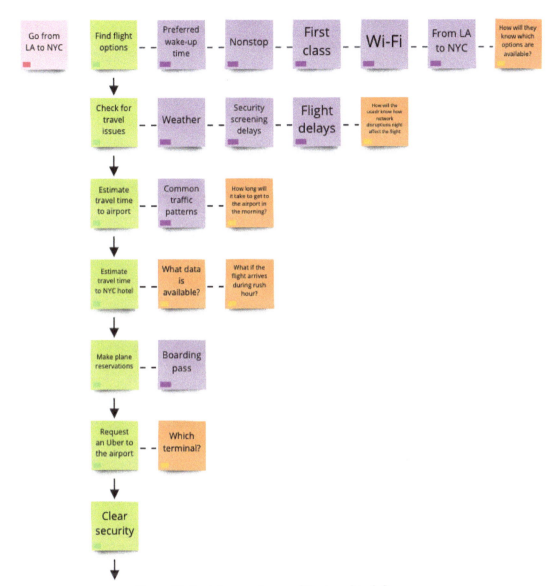

Figure 31: Part 1, second pass of the travel task flow.

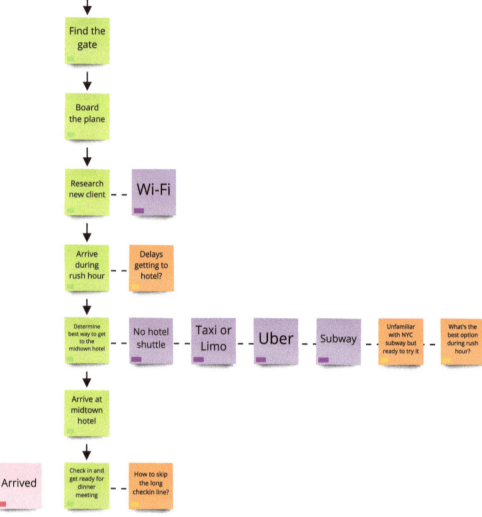

Figure 32: Part 2, second pass of the travel example task flow.

Travel Task Flow, Second Pass:

- **Misc:** Go from LA to NYC. **User:** Find flight options. **Artifact:** Preferred wake-up time, Nonstop, First class, Wi-Fi, From LA to NYC. **Issue:** How will they know which options are available?

- **User:** Check for travel issues. **Artifact:** Weather, Security screening delays, Flight delays. **Issue:** How will the user know how network disruptions might affect the flight?

- **User:** Estimate travel time to airport. **Artifact:** Common traffic patterns. **Issue:** How long will it take to get to the airport in the morning?

- **User:** Estimate travel time to NYC hotel. **Issue:** What data is available? What if the flight arrives during rush hour?

- **User:** Make plane reservations. **Artifact:** Boarding pass (within 24 hours of departure).

- **User:** Request an Uber® to the airport. **Issue:** Which terminal?

- **User:** Clear security.

- **User:** Find the gate.

- **User:** Board the plane.

- **User:** Research new client. **Artifact:** Wi-Fi.

- **User:** Arrive during rush hour. **Issue:** Delays getting to hotel?

- **User:** Determine best way to get to the midtown hotel. **Artifact:** No hotel shuttle, Taxi or limo, Uber, Subway. **Issue:** Unfamiliar with NYC subway, but ready to try it, What's the best option during rush hour?

- **User:** Arrive at midtown hotel.

- **Misc:** Arrived. **User:** Check in to hotel and get ready for dinner meeting. **Issue:** How to skip the long check-in line?

User Knowledge Profile

The user knowledge profile needs to capture the knowledge components of the intended user. There may be several different user types for this example scenario, but this is the main user knowledge profile that fits this scenario. The knowledge components of this user profile are:

- **Trigger.** Unexpected client dinner in New York City.

- **Desired outcome.** Must be there, refreshed, and ready to meet a new client for dinner in midtown.

- **Common knowledge.** Knows how to use different travel methods and sites. Knows to not rent a car in NYC.

- **Required knowledge.** Which NYC airport to fly into, which hotels are in midtown, how to get from NYC airport to midtown.

- **Knowledge gap.** Has never been to NYC and doesn't know how to get from the airport to their hotel in midtown Manhattan.

Traveler User Knowledge Profile

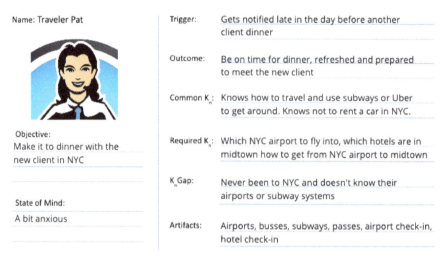

Figure 33: The user knowledge profile for Pat.

Turning Greens to Yellows

Make the system do more of the work by replacing the green sticky notes (user actions) with yellow sticky notes (system actions). You are removing user actions, streamlining the process, removing negative Task Dimensions, and having the system do more of the work for the user. You are dramatically reducing user efforts, errors, and the dependency to complete the task with the existing user knowledge, and you are promoting a best-practice approach to performing the task.

The following simplified example travel tasks flow demonstrates how an optimized task can be used to create an activity flow diagram that captures the actions required to achieve the desired outcome.

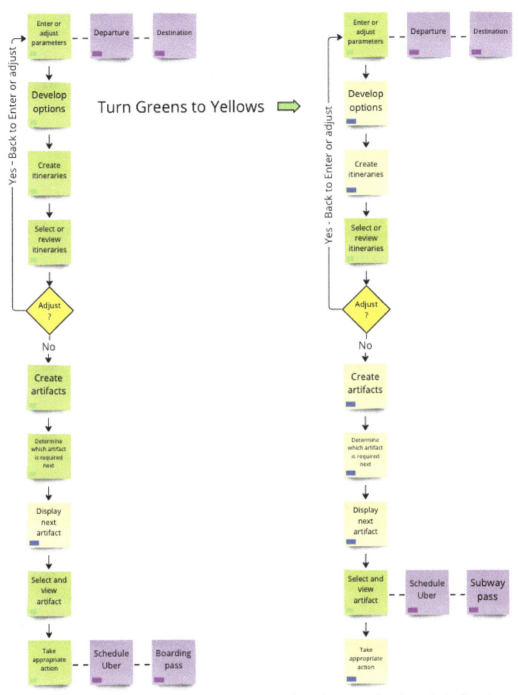

Figure 34: A simplified example travel task flow (second pass) compared to the optimized version illustrating the difference between the two.

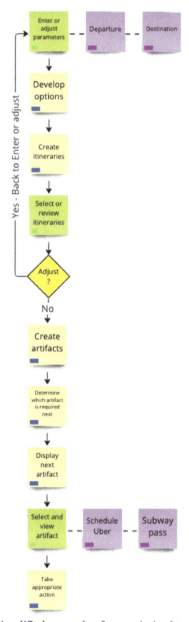

Figure 35: A simplified example of an optimized travel task flow.

A simplified example of the travel task flow, Optimized:

- **User:** Enter or adjust parameters. **Artifact:** Departure, Destination.

- **System:** Develop options.

- **System:** Create itineraries.

- **User:** Select or review itineraries.

- **Decision:** Adjust? **Yes:** back to Enter or adjust parameters. **No:** go to next step.

- **System:** Create artifacts.

- **System:** Determine which artifact is required next.

- **System:** Display next artifact.

- **User:** Select and view artifact. **Artifact:** Schedule Uber, Subway pass.

- **System:** Take appropriate action.

This diagram is a rough draft version of an optimized flow to illustrate how much of the task can be performed by the system. The next task flow image illustrates how this rough draft expands and changes when adding more detail to complete the task optimization.

The following diagram illustrates a more detailed version of the optimized task flow for Pat.

Travel Task Flow, Optimized

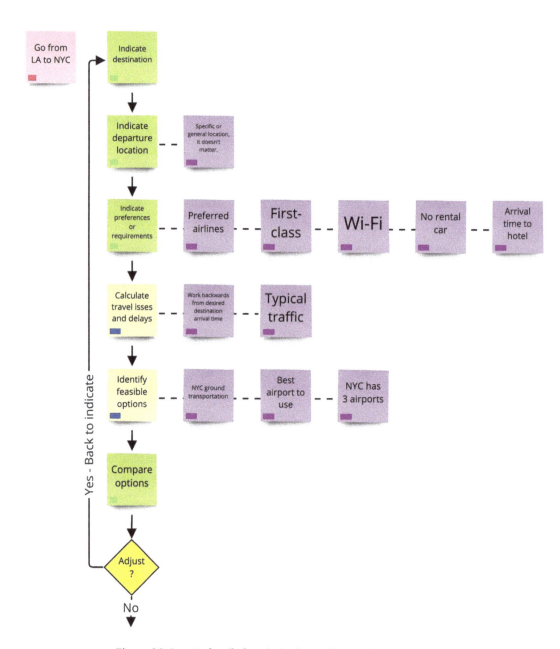

Figure 36: Part 1, detailed optimized travel example task flow.

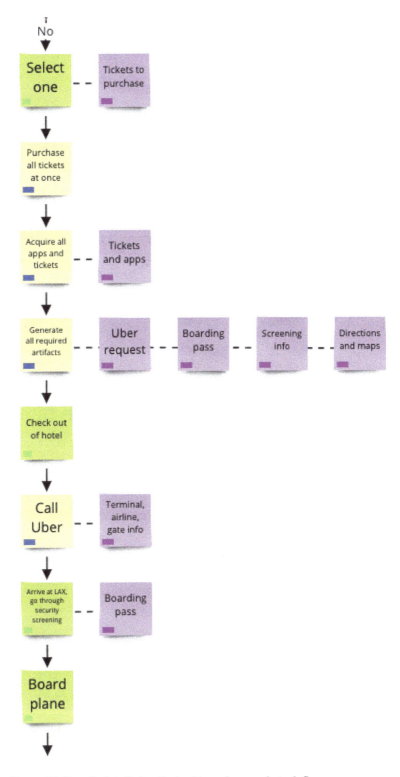

Figure 37: Part 2, detailed optimized travel example task flow.

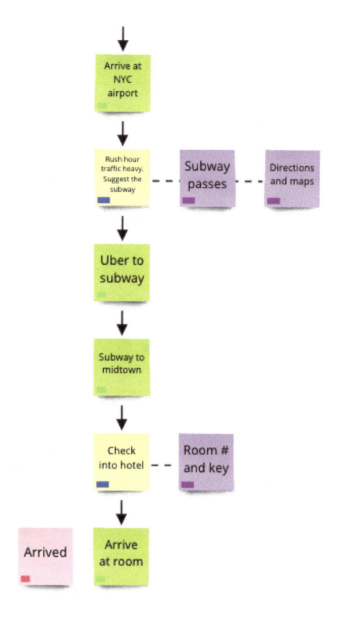

Figure 38: Part 3, detailed optimized travel example task flow.

Figure 39: Legend of the sticky note colors: User (green), System (yellow), Issue (orange), Artifact (purple), Misc (pink).

Travel Task Flow, Optimized:

- **Misc:** Go from LA to NYC. **User:** Indicate destination.

- **User:** Indicate departure location. **Artifact:** Specific or general location, it doesn't matter.

- **User:** Indicate preferences or requirements. **Artifact:** Preferred airlines, First class, Wi-Fi, No rental car, Arrival time to hotel.

- **System:** Calculate travel issues and delays. **Artifact:** Work backwards from desired destination arrival time, Typical traffic.

- **System:** Identify feasible options. **Artifact:** NYC ground transportation, Best airport to use, NYC has 3 airports.

- **User:** Compare options.

- **Decision:** Adjust? **Yes:** back to Indicate destination. **No:** go to next step.

- **User:** Select one. **Artifact:** Tickets to purchase.

- **System:** Purchase all tickets at once.

- **System:** Acquire all apps and tickets. **Artifact:** Tickets and apps.

- **System:** Generate all required artifacts. **Artifact:** Uber request, Boarding pass, Screening info, Directions and maps.

- **User:** Check out of hotel.

- **System:** Call Uber. **Artifact:** Terminal, airline, gate info.

- **User:** Arrive at LAX, go through security screening. **Artifact:** Boarding pass.

- **User:** Board plane.

- **User:** Arrive at NYC airport.

- **System:** Rush hour traffic heavy, suggest the subway. **Artifact:** Subway passes, Directions and maps.

- **User:** Uber to subway.

- **User:** Subway to midtown.

- **System:** Check into hotel. **Artifact:** Room # and key.

- **Misc:** Arrived. **User:** Arrive at room.

Task analysis is the key to creating knowledge-oriented designs. It provides a clear definition of who the users are and how they will flow through their tasks. It accurately identifies:

- The knowledge elements to embed into the design to help users perform their tasks.

- The actions the system should perform for the users.

- Which interfaces the users will need.

These can replace typical feature-oriented design requests or requirements, and help the team focus on the users. The next sections describe how to help the designers narrow in on the best possible solutions.

Getting More Buy-In for Task Analysis

Describe the high-level task flows. Provide just enough detail to describe how the user might go about solving their problem. Too much detail can confuse or overwhelm the non-UX folks in your company, who are only casually participating or observing this effort.

Share copies of these representative, high-level task flows on the wall, and ask folks for their comments, questions, and perspectives. Include the identified artifacts, knowledge, and questions in these flows too. This invited feedback makes the tasks more personally relevant and gives time for people to assimilate and think in terms of tasks rather than features.

Remember, **you** are the voice of the user and lead this effort. You determine which of the comments, questions, or perspectives fit this effort and which do not.

Getting More Buy-In for User Knowledge Profiles

Giving the profiles light-hearted names like Birthday Bob, Browsing Betty, and Surgical Shopper Sam helps folks learn to associate the task with the knowledge profile. For example, these three names refer to three potential ecommerce shopper profiles. Help them become familiar to the team throughout the project.

Given the tightly coupled relationship to the tasks, it's possible to combine the task flow and user knowledge profile descriptions into one conversation with the stakeholders.

Posting these user descriptions around the company, complete with caricature drawings to depict them (if possible), will influence everyone's belief in them. You might start hearing people refer to your light-hearted user profile names, like "Forgetful Frank," instead of just calling them "the user."

Getting More Buy-in for Task Optimization

An optimized task flow should look very different from the original. Include the details about the specific problem this optimized flow is trying to solve, how it reduces a dependency on user knowledge and skill, and how it leverages the company's knowledge.

Share a cleaned-up version of this task flow on the shared wall. By this time, people will be intrigued by the progress of the UX effort and will begin to understand how different a UX and Human-Centered research and design method is from typical UI and graphic design processes.

This is a good place to indicate how this optimized task benefits the business. The benefits vary from project to project, and are derived from the analysis, so there is no single formula for defining the value. It might be something about increasing relevance to more users, thus creating conversions, or that it better differentiates the product from the competitors. Regardless of which value you focus on, it should be specific enough to describe how this optimized task flow increases value for the business and helps the business achieve its goals.

Chapter 7:   Artifact Continuity

In typical UX efforts, personas, journey maps, empathy maps, etc., often aren't cross-referenced to one another, or lack continuity or consistency. In contrast, the knowledge-oriented UX process creates a series of linked artifacts (task flows, user knowledge profiles, etc.) that each directly and explicitly influence the next phase of the process and its artifacts.

Typical UX processes can seem "disconnected." Time and effort are sometimes spent creating artifacts that have little to do with the actual design. For example, it's an oft-heard complaint that UX teams spend weeks creating personas and then never really use them; they end up as artifacts stuck in a drawer, largely neglected once they've been created.

Unfortunately, the same holds true for many other artifacts, especially canvases and exercises used in workshops and design-by-committee adventures. Teams might create personas, empathy maps, How Might We statements, journey maps, and so on, but these artifacts were often created from guesses or brainstorming, rather than from deep knowledge of customers, systems, and context generated from qualitative research.

Did these artifacts inform or influence the design, strategy, or direction of the product? Probably not. Meaningful and actionable artifacts should influence strategies, decisions, and products. Moreover, if these artifacts were really that useful, why are there still so many mediocre designs based on them?

Why do these artifacts fail to deliver exemplary results? Two main reasons:

1. **How the artifacts were made.** It's not UX without the "U," or users, yet many companies and teams create UX artifacts, such as personas and customer journey maps, from guesses and assumptions. They are certain they "know" their customers, but what are the chances they are wrong, even a little? And what risk does this create?

2. **Well-made artifacts can still deliver poor results if they don't directly influence the next step of the UX process.** With our critical thinking hats on, we can ask ourselves *How does a persona influence the prioritization of features? How does the empathy map influence the design strategy? What will we do differently because of what we "believe" people feel? Was our actual design directly influenced by our strategy? Or did our design strategy get forgotten somewhere along the way?* And so on.

For example, think about how empathy maps are described and used in many UX courses and team workshops, and then ask some critical thinking questions about that artifact:

- We can observe what people do or say, but how do we *know* what users think or feel? Were those guesses or assumptions based on stereotypes of the intended user group?

- Have we entered into high-ego territory by imagining that we truly know what another person or group of people think or feel?

- What is our definition of "empathy"? Many would incorrectly say that it's "thinking about our users." Cognitive empathy goes beyond the intellectual exercise of thinking about someone you don't know or understand. Cognitive empathy is about understanding people's realities, perspectives, and needs from their perspectives no matter what you believe, think, or would choose for those people. It's about putting yourself and what you prefer aside to deliver what best matches your target audience.

- Can great and innovative products be designed if we felt sympathy for users' experiences and took action, but never felt empathy?

- What would be different in our workflow if we never made an empathy map?

- If the goal of an empathy map is to help teammates understand customers, does the empathy map achieve that? Could something else achieve that more effectively?

- What are some other artifacts that our UX team can deliver that would serve the same purpose the empathy map claims to achieve (understanding customers)? Would better personas (user knowledge profiles), video montages from research, or direct quotes from participants tell the story better?

- Will our team keep that empathy map by our side as we work on the information architecture or interaction design?

- How does an empathy map directly or explicitly influence a design decision?

Connected Artifacts

In knowledge-oriented UX, each step directly relates to, influences, informs, and connects to the next step, from research to design to testing. It also suggests how the research can inform business and marketing strategies.

Without a direct linkage from one artifact to the next, the process would rely on various team members to interpret each artifact, translate, and transfer the salient points to the next artifact. Even when that information is transferred in a report or presentation, there is still the potential for misinterpretation.

A process that more tightly couples the result of one step to the beginning of the next ensures that the work done in each step directly supports the entire effort. When each artifact directly links to the next process step and artifact, there is no interpretation required. The UX methods described in this book provide a holistic, continuous process that reduces the reliance on data interpretation, and avoids the problems of typical disjointed methods and their artifacts.

The example travel problem demonstrates how each artifact is connected to the others. The observations and interviews in this process result in task flows that identify the data which directly contribute to the user knowledge profile. In turn, the profile informs the task optimization, which, when combined with the company's knowledge artifacts, drives the design to solve the users' unmet needs and bridge the knowledge gap. Additionally, the task analysis influences the test tasks for usability testing.

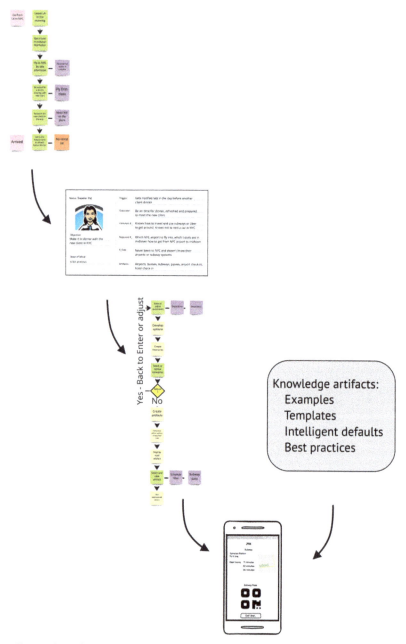

Figure 40: Illustration of how the task flow leads to the user knowledge profile, which then leads to the optimized task flow, which leads to the design, which is also guided by the knowledge artifacts.

Task Analysis vs. Jobs To Be Done® (JTBD)

If you are familiar with JTBD, now that you have learned more about knowledge-oriented design, you can start to see the differences.

"Jobs To Be Done" is a popular framework that starts us on a path toward being more user-centered, but often lacks the detail that task analysis and knowledge-oriented methods deliver.

Both JTBD and task analysis seek to focus teams and projects on the objectives and goals our users and customers have. Both require you to be familiar with your target audiences' behaviors and needs in a solution-agnostic way. This makes them similar "concepts," but their execution is quite different.

Some JTBD authors and trainers declare that research is optional. *You can work from current knowledge or current assumptions about users.* Some JTBD fans suggest that any type of research done by anybody at the company is "good enough," even if that research isn't observational or the right method for what we need to learn.

Based on how JTBD is often presented, it appears to be a derivative of task analysis. It is often a "smaller" method with less detail, which can make it less actionable.

JTBD often jumps from the job statement to one or more solution concepts. For example, Pat's Job To Be Done is to get from LA to a NYC meeting on time. There are many solutions that would achieve this, from working with a human travel agent to using an aggregator website like Kayak®. But when we consider what we learned about the details of Pat's task, such as their tools, knowledge, workarounds, and mental model, are these the best solutions?

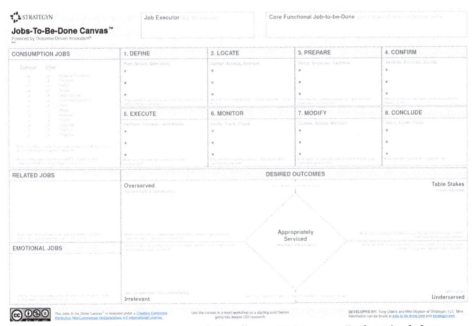

Figure 41: The Strategyn.com website offers a JTBD canvas. Explanation below.

The JTBD canvas from Strategyn.com asks for information such as which aspects of getting the job done must be defined by the customer up front, which items do they need to locate, how does the customer prepare their environment, and what must the customer verify before proceeding to ensure success.

It's hard to complete Pat's travel example with JTBD. Give it a try! Pat's key problem isn't necessarily the task environment or items they need to locate. What will make or break Pat's experience and task is **knowledge**. Without a system that takes the knowledge work off of Pat's shoulders, they will need to quickly become very familiar with NYC geography and mass transit. If we didn't consider this knowledge gap in our research, strategy, and design work, we might end up designing for Pat's "Job." We'll get Pat to New York City, but can we significantly improve their task? Can we reduce their likelihood of errors and the massive cognitive load of NYC travel?

This is where knowledge-oriented UX (including task analysis) and JTBD diverge. Ultimately, using a Jobs To Be Done paradigm is better than having no customer-centric or user-focused approach at all. If your company is already familiar with JTBD, evolving into task analysis will be easier. If your company is unfamiliar with task analysis, you don't need JTBD as a stepping stone.

PART 4: DEFINE THE UX STRATEGY

Chapter 8: A Well-Crafted Strategy

Even though UX teams typically create design briefs, empathy maps, personas, and other common artifacts, many of them neglect to create a UX strategy. A UX strategy does not refer to the company's organization or processes, but the focus of the interaction model and interface design. It provides an overarching direction or goal that the design should achieve. It often impacts more than just the design, but influences how the direction of the business and marketing efforts as well.

In the ProFlowers case study, the research identified that the users didn't know much about flowers; they only knew why they needed them, for a specific occasion. It was all about the occasion. Thus, the UX strategy became "ProFlowers doesn't sell flowers. They sell occasions." This strategy drove the design to organize the flowers by occasion rather than flower type, which was the common approach by the main competitors.

A good UX strategy should drive all of the design decisions for the project. It should be described well enough that everyone is clear on what direction the design should go. This is more than just simply restating the KPIs. A strategy is more about *how* the design will achieve those KPIs.

A common objective of business-to-business (B2B) websites is to generate leads. Most sites are designed to offer lots of content in the hopes that users will call the company or sign up for a sales demo. These types of sites expect the user to be impressed by all of the literature, but it typically doesn't work that well. These digital brochures rely on users reading, understanding, and assimilating all of the information. Users would then have to determine if the company or product is a good fit for their problem, as they understand it.

A better approach is for the website to demonstrate domain knowledge by listing a handful of key problems most customers have, and then organizing the relevant material relative to each problem. This might mean duplicating information so that people following the content related to their problem get the information they need without being told to read a FAQ or jump to another page about another problem.

Thus, a strategy might be that the site should behave like a **consultant** rather than a brochure. A consultant uses their knowledge and experience to provide questions that identify the user's need, and then offer information relative to that need. As has been described, a brochure relies on users reading everything and deciding, usually without the right knowledge, what to do.

By helping users identify their problem or need, the site can then provide a specific solution path that mimics how a personal consultant might address the problem.

A good user experience can make up for a bad design better than a good design can make up for a bad user experience. Users would rather have relevant content and a streamlined experience than a pretty interface.

After President Kennedy's famous speech about going to the moon, asking anyone at NASA—an astronaut, a flight engineer, even a janitor pushing a broom down the hall—"What are you doing?" would result in the same answer: "We're going to the moon." That single, shared visionary statement guided all of their activities. Every project needs just such a shared goal or perspective.

What does a good strategy look like? Let's start with what it *doesn't* look like:

- **Anything non-user-centered such as "increasing revenue," "more conversions," or "more engagement."** Any plan to guide or push users to serve the needs of the business isn't a strategy. These are typical business goals, but they don't address a problem the *user* is trying to solve.

- **Anything that prescribes the solution.** For example, "Users need a dashboard," or, "We need a button that will…"

- **Any guesses about the causes of problems if we haven't learned root causes from recent generative research.** For example, statements of opinion unverified by research, such as, "Users are/aren't doing X, probably because Y."

- **Reliance solely on quantitative data.** For example, "28% of mobile web users aren't filtering search results. Therefore, there must be a problem with mobile search filtering." This sounds like 28% of users decided not to filter results for unknown reasons that could range from *laziness* to *they were happy with search results and didn't need to filter*. Qualitative research data would indicate if there is a problem here and what those problems are.

The strategy must relate to the user, not the business. For example, the ProFlowers objective was clearly defined as, "Users must be able to find the right flowers for their occasion."

A well-crafted strategy will resonate with the users' needs or problems. One project I worked on involved the status report generated by a blood analyzer device at the end of a complex blood screening process. The report was used to identify any contaminated units of blood that should be destroyed, and to give authorization for the rest of the units of blood to be released. Blood screening directors were more concerned that the process had been followed accurately and no vials were mixed up, than they were about the readability of the report.

The strategy wasn't to create a better report, it was to give the lab directors confidence that they weren't going to mistakenly release contaminated blood to any patients. This strategy completely changed the project from just focusing on improving the report to creating software that tracked each vial during the complex blood screening process.

Crafting a UX Strategy

Achieving a user-oriented strategy relies on the insights from the research and analysis, which are then used to pivot the business to benefit from serving those user objectives. Great research around people, systems, and context will identify unmet user needs, which the business can leverage to build strategies and initiatives.

Crafting a good strategy involves answering questions like the following:

- What problem are the users trying to solve?

- How do they try to solve it now?

- What does the desired outcome look like?

- How can the business also benefit from solving that problem?

Crafting a good strategy relies on identifying the user's objective and describing a desired end state. Find a way to characterize the desired outcome in a focused but nonspecific, solution-agnostic way. Such a strategy statement will leave room for innovating different solution approaches. Note that users' objectives are often different from business objectives: it's okay if they don't completely align.

For example, in the ProFlowers case, the original business objective was to increase conversion rates and encourage users to buy more flowers. The user's problem wasn't to "buy more flowers," it was around recognizing a special occasion. The objective was redefined as *helping users find the right bouquet that addressed a specific occasion.*

A good strategy will be singularly focused on the product's and user's key objective. A good metric is to focus on the top 90%-95% of the problems users need help with. That typically is only about five to ten actual problems. Trying to solve too many problems is a clear indication that the product lacks a single, cohesive strategy and will inevitably fail.

This is a relatively difficult process that relies on practice and experience. It requires deep critical thinking to identify that aspect of the users' problem that lends itself to defining the solution approach.

Consider the users' perception of their problem and what limits their ability to solve it on their own. Then find a way to describe how the design could help the user solve their problem. One method is to think of the system as some type of agent for the user.

Some example strategies:

- Be a personal shopper, rather than just an ecommerce site.

- Be a medical assistant, rather than just a medical info site.

- Be a pilot scheduler, rather than a calendar app.

Find a way to describe a design strategy that suggests the system or company will do more of the work for the user. Try to imagine how knowledge could be applied to help the user in the least demanding way. Think of ways to describe the strategy as a human, or robot, or anything that does not rely on the user doing all of the work.

The Vanguard Story

In their first attempt at a self-service investment management website, Vanguard® Mutual Funds created a site design that reflected the business silos within their organization. Each of the investment vehicles had its own site, such as mutual funds, stocks, bonds, etc. Users with multiple investment holdings were required to visit each silo separately to see the value of each investment. The website did not organize the user's holdings in any form, requiring users to find their specific investments and add them up on spreadsheets or paper. Many of the users were a bit older and not necessarily tech savvy enough to create such a spreadsheet.

The website was a mostly static display of individual valuations that depended on the user performing all of the work to ascertain their progress towards their investment objective.

This frustrated the users and generated exorbitant support costs that diluted the intended cost benefits of the website. Vanguard wanted a site that fully supported their customers' needs without taxing customer support representatives.

I conducted observational research with dozens of users that identified that the typical investor held multiple types of investment instruments in various combinations, depending on their investment objectives. Each objective had a different investment profile. For example, a mid-career couple might each have several investment objectives and profiles, such as:

- Individual retirement portfolios that included conservative investments like mutual funds and blue-chip stocks.
- A semi-aggressive college fund with stocks, bonds, and money market holdings.
- A more aggressive vacation home savings plan with other stocks, money market funds, etc.

Users had difficulty navigating the 16,000 pages of the Vanguard website. Given the similarities of cryptic mutual fund and stock names, users weren't always sure they found the right data. The spot prices they were shown did not indicate the progress towards their investment goals. This confusion caused undesirable consequences, such as

---

customers unknowingly buying stocks that were already part of one of their mutual funds, which over-exposed them to that stock.

The UX strategy was to turn the site into a wealth management center that collated all of a customer's holdings into separate portfolios based on their *objectives*. Plot the progress of each portfolio, and suggest action items to address any anomalies, such as reducing exposure to specific stocks. The strategy became to "create a digital wealth management advisor." This solution has been in place for over 20 years and has become the de facto interaction model for other major investment firms.

Demonstrating the Business Value of Solving User Problems

Our strategy is user-focused, but we must be able to show the business the values and benefits of solving users' problems. There is unfortunately a good chance that if you tell leaders or stakeholders that users are experiencing a certain problem, they might not care. Despite all of the "empathy" going around, solving this problem or unmet need might not be considered a priority.

Our UX strategy highlights the *whys*: why would we do this project? Which problems can we solve for users? Which goals can we help the business achieve while living up to our company values and brand promise in the eyes of the users? How will we balance business and user needs, and create win-wins?

We might consider communicating these via a traditional impact map or similar tree that claims to detail opportunities or solutions, but they have some clear disadvantages.

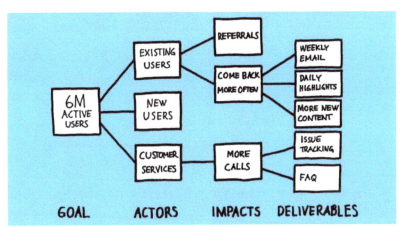

Figure 42: Sample impact map showing how we'll reach six million active users. The impacts are "referrals" and "come back more often." The deliverables are "weekly emails," "daily highlights," and "more new content."

This approach to impact mapping has some weaknesses:

- **We started with a *business* goal.** Our decisions and actions will be driven by achieving that business goal. If the business goal was not influenced by great research insights, we might have a business goal unrelated to or even working against users' needs.

- **We built a map based on how we can push users toward our business goal.** Where is the value to the users? Why should they increase their purchase frequency or view more ads? Is that what they would choose for themselves?

- **Solution assumptions.** How do we know that a better layout will create the desired impact? How do we know that offering more discounts, weekly emails, or "more content" will achieve our ultimate business goal? Do we know which content types or topics will be most effective?

- **We didn't map user problems or tasks.** If a template doesn't include users' problems, pain points, or unmet needs, we are unlikely to find user-centered solutions.

What if we created an impact map where the goal is something our users are trying to achieve, and then we tied that to business value?

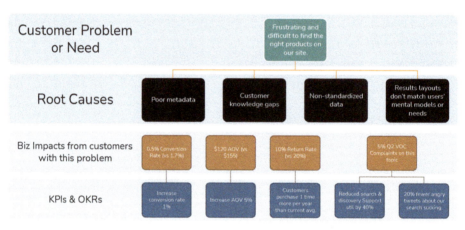

Figure 43: Sample Delta CX Impact Map. Explained below.

Our key customer or user problem or need is at the top of Debbie Levitt's Delta CX Impact Map. The example used above is "frustrating and difficult to find the right products on our site." The next level of the map indicates some of the root causes creating or aggravating this problem. For this sample map, these causes are poor metadata, user knowledge gaps, non-standardized data (sometimes entered by third parties), and the layout of the results not matching users' mental models or needs (perhaps they prefer a grid over a list).

We next document the impact on the business. *Users are suffering, and here is how that plays out for our project or company.* For this sample map, the business impacts are a lower conversion rate (0.5% for customers struggling with search results versus 1.7% for our general population), lower Average Order Value (AOV of $120 versus $155), 10% returning customer visit rate (versus 20%), and increased VOC complaints (5% of our Q2 complaints were about this topic). Include any numbers or estimates you have, especially around lost revenue. Note that visually, the tree breaks between the root causes and the business impacts since there isn't a one-to-one relationship. Many root causes are affecting many business impacts.

Since the Delta CX Impact Map doesn't focus on potential solutions, the final level of the tree indicates KPIs and OKRs that will show when we have improved or resolved this problem for our users. Metrics might include an increased conversion rate, increased AOV, customers purchasing more frequently than average, and reduced utilization of Customer Support channels related to this problem.

This approach to impact mapping allows us to focus on the user while considering how the problem impacts both users and the business. We can summarize root causes to indicate that we generally understand where we might focus potential solutions, but the map is solution-agnostic. Ultimately, if we can repair the root causes and resolve the original user problem or need, we will see gains and improvements in both business-related and user-related metrics.

We rarely get project buy-in because stakeholders and leaders deeply care about solving users' problems. This impact mapping style allows us to tie a user need or opportunity to how it will achieve business goals or begin to fix business problems like loss of revenue and low customer loyalty.

Prioritization/Viability Matrix

Function/Task	User Experience	Business	Tech. Feasibility	Overall
Duplication of effort	3	3	3	9
Low tech transfer of data	3	3	3	9
Tie events to anomalies	2	3	2	7
Outsourced Strong Admin/Teacher (reminders)	3	3	1	7
Intelligent default thresholds	1	2	1	4
Standardized Reports	1	1	1	3
Progress to Mandates/Drivers/plans	2	1	2	5
Who has the info?	2	2	1	5
Data input payback? (motivation to supply data)	3	2	3	8
Track events & results (campaigns)	2	3	2	7
Annotating reports/results (explain spikes)	2	3	2	7
Dashboard (real-time, trends, exceptions)	1	1	1	3
Fresh content (visibility)	2	1	1	4
Best practices (knowledge)	1	2	2	5
Profile matching	2	1	3	6
Unit Conversion	1	1	1	3
Setting Reasonable Goals (walls)	1	1	3	5
Calculated/Suggested targets	1	1	2	4
Projections	2	1	3	6
Project Library	2	1	2	5
Prioritizations	2	2	3	7
Pilot testing	3	3	3	9
Change culture/perception/behaviors	3	3	3	9
Longitudinal history/progress	1	2	1	4
Survey management	3	2	2	7
Selling to administration	3	2	2	7
Student Communication suite (visibility)	1	3	2	6
Updated policy/reporting requirements	3	2	3	8
Idea capture/sim-sustain/trivia	1	3	1	5
Suggested student projects	3	3	2	8
What-if tool (compare projects)	2	2	1	5
				0
Distribution: 1s	10	10	10	
2s	11	10	11	
3s	10	11	10	

Figure 44: A completed matrix with green bars indicating the highest priority (lowest score) tasks.

The priority matrix marks the transition from the research phase into the design phase and objectively identifies the best return-on-investment (ROI) design opportunities as well as the low-hanging fruit, based on a balance of the business objectives, user needs, and technical feasibility. If this is a new product, this helps determine which tasks to support and features to include in version 1.0.

This section describes a disciplined method of identifying and balancing the competing priorities of the users' needs, business and marketing objectives, and technical feasibility. The result of this exercise is a prioritized list of tasks that represent the most important user objectives for the product.

This process is a group effort and relies on a representative from each of the three described perspectives. If possible, have two or three people represent each perspective:

- User needs are represented by UX researchers.

- Business and marketing objectives are represented by business and marketing representatives and product managers. This perspective can also be represented by other roles, such as product development manager, product owner, business analyst, marketing, product marketing managers, and business executives.

- Technology is represented by the engineering or development leads. This perspective is often represented by the lead engineer or developer, or an engineering manager, someone knowledgeable about the technology they currently have and familiar with what's feasible.

  o This is the most complicated column to rank, because there are many factors and dependencies that determine how feasible a specific technology approach might be. Don't be surprised if this sparks long conversations.

The goal is to identify the priorities in each of the perspectives, and then combine them to create an overall score that determines which tasks and elements to design for first, and which ones can wait.

Rather than prioritizing a list of features, the matrix focuses on specific user tasks, which will be supported by a collection of features. Prioritizing user tasks rather than features avoids feature gaps that would make it difficult for the users to complete a specific task. Many designs provide features, but starting with a feature list might leave out or deprioritize some of the features that would support a complete task, leaving gaps in the task flow.

The tasks are identified in the task analysis phase of the UX effort. Users strive to achieve a desired outcome by performing those tasks. People don't want to use features; they want to complete a task. A famous quote in marketing comes from Harvard Business School Professor Theodore Levitt: "People don't want a quarter-inch drill; they want a quarter-inch hole!"

Representatives from the users, business, and technical perspectives rank each task on a priority scale of 1 (highest) to 3 (lowest). It's important to have each perspective complete their rankings on a blank matrix while hiding the scores from the other perspectives to avoid them being influenced by other scores. There will inevitably be discussions or debates, but this is a good thing. During this cross-discipline exercise, keep notes of the conversations. These discussions can educate various stakeholders about the priorities of the other perspectives, which improves the eventual design.

Adding the individual scores produces a combined score that suggests which tasks deserve the primary attention, and which ones can be addressed later. **The lowest scoring tasks, shown as the highlight rows (dark green in figure 42), must be addressed first, as these are your highest priorities.** The higher scoring tasks may not be addressed right away, but at least you know they are in the potential future. You can ensure that you don't create a design that ultimately prevents those tasks.

The "User Needs" or "User Experience" column consists of the rated importance of each task with respect to how it supports the users' needs. This perspective is represented by the UX researcher and is based on the data cultivated from the observational research. Score a task a 1 if it is necessary to achieve the users' objective. Score it a 2 if it supports a necessary task, and a 3 if it is something that can wait.

It is best to conduct this prioritization prior to the meeting, and then wait to share these scores until after the scoring for the other two perspectives is completed. Since it's quite likely that these values are not accurate yet, they are open for discussion among the research team for further refinement. Discussion of the user experience values should occur in meetings of the researchers separately from the business, marketing, and development teams. Once the values have been determined, then it's okay to convene the prioritization/viability meeting.

The "Business and Marketing Objectives" or "Business" column contains the ratings of the importance of this task to business or marketing objectives. How well does this task help accomplish the company's strategic goals or marketing initiatives? If a task is a "must have" or directly supports a key objective, score it as 1. If it's a supporting task, score it as 2. If it can wait, score it as 3.

The Technical Feasibility column ranks the ease of providing the technical capabilities related to the task. A score of 1 indicates something easier to implement, and 3 is more difficult. This column can also be ranked by whether the technical capabilities already exist or by the amount of effort it would take to deliver them. If most or all of the capabilities already exist, then score it as a 1. If some exist, but others require development or modification, then it's a 2. If most or all of a capability does not exist, then it's a 3.

Remember that this matrix is only a guideline. There may be other factors not captured in this matrix that affect the ranking. For example, if a feature appears in multiple tasks including higher priority ones, it could affect the feasibility ranking of a lower priority task that uses that same feature. It is useful to capture these dependencies and relationships.

The key to this priority matrix's success is pushing everyone to be honest about priorities. It's common for marketing to make everything a 1 and technology to make everything a 3. To account for this, each perspective must equally distribute their 1s, 2s, and 3s. The matrix only works by forcing equal distribution within each column, otherwise the team cannot achieve a truly accurate prioritization scheme. For example, if there are 15 items in your matrix, then each perspective can use five 1s, five 2s, and five 3s.

Regardless of how much you may believe that 9 out of 15 items seem to qualify as a 1, you must determine which 4 of those need to be relegated to a lower score. The scoring is not necessarily based on an absolute scale, it is more of a relative scale. You must have equal distribution of the scores.

Once everybody has established the rankings for their domain, calculate the final scores for each task. The best possible combined score for a task is 3, when all three perspectives have scored it a 1. The worst possible score is 9, when all three perspectives scored this task a 3. Note that like golf, the lower number is the better score. Conversely, the items with the larger numeric totals are the lower priority. There should be an almost equal distribution of low, medium, and high scores.

This creates a guideline for prioritization. Start by focusing on the tasks that scored 3 or 4. Subsequent design efforts should focus on all of the 5s and 6s, and possibly some of the 7s. Designs should plan for all of the listed tasks, including the 8s and 9s, since we will have them on our roadmap. We don't want to design for the *now* without considering the *next* as well.

Once the scores have been determined, hold a group meeting to discuss the outcome of the exercise. This will likely foster open discussions about the discovered issues, and we welcome those. There will likely be tradeoffs that impact the priorities, which must be addressed in the group meeting.

One of the valuable side effects of completing this matrix is the deeper understanding each group has for the other perspectives. The techies learn why the business wants a particular task included in the design. The business learns why some things are more difficult to develop. Sometimes engineers prefer to build the easier features first, but that might leave little time for a more difficult but higher-business-priority task. The shared understanding promoted by this effort helps ensure that everyone is on the same page about the product direction.

Function/Task	User Experience	Business	Tech Feasibility	Overall
Find right flowers for an occasion	1	1	3	5
Add to cart	3	3	1	7
Include personal note	1	2	3	6
Provide payment	3	2	1	6
Provide shipping address	2	3	2	7
Don't forget, again	2	1	2	5
Distribution: 1s	2	2	2	
2s	2	2	2	
3s	2	2	2	

Figure 45: A simple version of the ProFlowers priority matrix.

The matrix shown here is a representative subset of the actual matrix and illustrates how the matrix identified the highest priority tasks. Finding the right flowers for the occasion is a key task for the users, and is central to the business objectives, thus earning a score of 1 for both. Despite it being technically challenging (score of 3), it still scored low enough to be a high enough priority to be included in first version of the design.

Note how even though it was technically feasible (score of 1) to provide a shopping cart, and yet the user and business perspectives rated it a score of 3. Despite it being easy to add into the design, the overall score of 7 suggested that the cart should be left out of the first version of the design effort so that the developers could use that time to work on higher priority tasks.

The ProFlowers case study provides a good example of task analysis and prioritization. Considering the low priority for "add to cart" with a score of 7, while common to pretty much every ecommerce site, the research indicated that customers typically buy only one bouquet. The research also identified that there are no shopping carts in brick-and-mortar florist shops. The priority matrix clearly identified that users didn't need a shopping cart, and thus the team eliminated that feature and avoided the unnecessary task of "adding to cart."

Moreover, eliminating the cart provided smoother upsell opportunities to the customer. "Would you want the flowers to arrive without a vase to put them in?" "Which vase do you think they would like?" Compare that to the typical uninspiring user experience of "find vase, select vase, add to cart, checkout cart."

Getting More Buy-In for Prioritization

If the prioritization matrix is included in your research process, post it on the wall with all of the dependencies and notes included. It helps to remind everyone that the matrix represents a guideline, not a hard and fast rule. It is only a plan from which to deviate.

The matrix also helps people understand the subsequent UX design strategy that the design team will follow. Describe the strategy and how it will inform the design approach based on the accepted priorities. This helps reduce the potential for people adding in the "what-if" type of features that tend to clutter a design.

Identifying and Aligning with the Right Mental Model

A mental model is the user's perception of how something works based on what the user can see or know about the product. A familiar example is the automatic transmission in an automobile. The user understands that to put the car in motion they just need to move the selector into Drive or Reverse and press the accelerator. They don't have to understand how the transmission actually works, which is very complicated and is not just two gears, drive and reverse. The mental model "hides" the complexity of the torque converter, modulator, and planetary gears from the user, and presents an understandable perception of how to make the car go.

A common inaccurate mental model is the electric stove. Many people mistakenly believe that the cooking burner will heat up faster if you turn the temperature dial all the way up to high. It doesn't. The stove supplies a constant amount of electricity to the burner no matter which temperature you select. It takes just as long for the burner to reach medium temperature whether you select medium or high on the dial. This inaccurate mental model is a carry-over from the mental model of the gas stove, which heats differently based on how much gas you give it. If you turn the dial to high, the burner gets more gas and heats up faster.

Part of research analysis includes identifying the right mental model that a design should suggest and align to. Users will develop a mental model based on the visual and interaction cues provided by the design, whether or not those cues were intentional. Users may also compare their mental models from previous experiences with other products; if there's too much of a disconnect, they may have trouble applying their existing mental model and struggle to use the product the first time, or even learning it at all.

Once the design priorities have been determined by analyzing the task flows, you should identify a mental model that suggests how the design should perform tasks. This should help guide the users' perceptions of how they should interact with the design. The mental model must be consistent with the user's understanding of the tasks and support the design strategy. Try to identify a mental model that the users already understand, using the suggestions in the next section.

A mental model is not usually the same as a UX strategy. The design strategy of the automatic transmission is to reduce the complexity of putting the car in gear. The mental model is a simple gear selector. The mental model and strategy are different but work together.

Although mental models are described at this point of the book, they may begin to surface at any time in the research and design process. Given their familiarity with the users and the stage of the research processes where mental models begin to surface, user researchers typically suggest mental models, though the designers may create designs that suggest them as well.

Read more about mental models in Don Norman's book, *The Design of Everyday Things*.

ProFlowers Mental Model Example

A common mental model for ecommerce sites is the shopping cart, which "holds" multiple items for purchase. Adding items to the cart is a familiar task. Since flower shops don't have shopping carts, and buyers typically purchase only one bouquet, the mental model was to check out as soon as they selected a bouquet.

Forcing users to "add to cart" and then "check out" from an online shopping cart added an unnecessary step to the process, making it more of a routine transaction than a meaningful experience. The cart treated the experience like any ordinary shopping task, which weakened the emotional aspect unique to this scenario.

The design decision was made to eliminate the shopping cart and reinforce the mental model of taking the bouquet straight to the counter. This proved highly successful, and provided opportunities to support suggestive selling, such as asking, "Do you want a vase with that bouquet?" This was much more engaging than relying on the user to know to look for a vase or teddy bear to add to the purchase.

Chapter 9:   Example Travel Project: Design Strategy

Most people don't plan their business travel like they might for vacation or personal travel. They have different priorities and objectives and need a different model. Rather than providing a design that relies on the user doing all of the work, create a system that identifies the travel parameters and preferences, and suggests various solutions. An effective design strategy here would be to create a travel tool that operates similarly to a company travel agent who presents options and adjusts the options based on the traveler's response to them. Think of how the traveler would interact with a travel agent and design for that type of "conversation."

Travel Project Priority Matrix

Function/Task	User Experience	Business	Tech Feasibility	Overall
Indicate destination	2			
Indicate departure location	2			
Indicate preferences/requirements	1			
Calculate traffic issues/delays	3			
Compare flights	2			
Compare hotels	3			
Compare itineraries/options	3			
Adjust itinerary details/preferences	2			
Select/purchase an itinerary	1			
Create itinerary artifacts	1			
Provide instructions	1			
Perform travel	3			
Check into hotel	2			
Distribution: 1s	4			
2s	5			
3s	4			

Figure 46: A sample prioritization matrix for the travel example, with UX priorities indicated. Note the even distribution of scores for the tasks.

Here is the travel project matrix with an initial pass of the user experience prioritization scores or values. Note the even distribution of scores.

Travel Mental Model

In the example project about Pat, who has to travel from Los Angeles to New York, what is their mental model?

An appropriate mental model should fit their expectation of what they would like the system to do for them and not just mimic existing tools. Existing travel websites tend to aggregate information from various sources without actually doing much to reduce the cognitive burden of the user. Pat would like a travel agent to search and compare the various travel options, and provide them with one single, best, most appropriate itinerary. When Pat agrees to it, the itinerary can be booked, all of the reservations made, and confirmation codes sent to their phone. In essence, a viable mental model would be a *digital travel agent*.

This "digital travel agent" mental model is solution-agnostic and addresses the root problem of this task domain: to efficiently identify an acceptable travel itinerary that considers all of the traveler's requirements and books the reservations for Pat.

Existing travel planning tools don't actually "plan" anything. They merely provide potential options for one part of the total travel problem. The user must still do all of the research, selection, and planning. A tool that actually *does* all of the planning and generates a workable itinerary is a very different mental model and user experience.

Getting More Buy-In for UX Design Strategy

This is the point where there is enough research insight to promote a shared understanding by the stakeholders regarding the direction the design should go—the potential UX design strategy. Some folks will begin to experience that all important "aha!" moment, recognizing that the research has uncovered a more worthwhile unmet need.

Share this strategy and the reasons for it (with respect to the unmet user needs). Don't be surprised to find interesting questions and additional suggestions, since this is a common point for people to start thinking differently about the design opportunities.

PART 5:   KNOWLEDGE DESIGN

Chapter 10: Designing Knowledge into the Product

Proper user research leads to more accurately defined problems. Since the best solutions solve *real* problems, it stands to reason that an accurately-defined problem produces a better, possibly unexpected solution.

If you haven't solved the right problem, what have you accomplished? How much time did that waste and what did it cost?

If your design looks and behaves similarly to everyone else's, then you have failed to identify the unique research insights that should have differentiated your solution from the others. Unique insights are just that: insights about the users' problems that are different from everyone else's. This goes beyond the surface level of UI design and refers to the overall solution strategy.

For example, if everyone else's website is a digital brochure and yours is also a digital brochure, you have failed to identify the true unmet need that will differentiate your design from the others. Consider how an interactive design that was more of a consultant to the user would be perceived and valued.

Knowledge design is a research and design approach I developed that focuses on identifying and embedding knowledge into a design to encourage user behaviors that make them succeed beyond their current skills and knowledge. Successful knowledge design should leverage the company's knowledge about a domain, product, service, or process to intentionally drive specific user actions that achieve the users' desired outcomes.

This is actually what User-Centered Design (UCD) was supposed to accomplish, but many people misunderstand UCD, and choose to work with derivatives that tend to be lesser in scope and outcomes. Here, and based on decades of experience, we evolved UCD to specifically include designing knowledge into the product or service.

Knowledge design isn't about bombarding users with "knowledge" or information like tutorials, tooltips, and instructional guidance; it's about filling the *knowledge gaps* we identify in this process with an intuitive design that guides users towards a successful result. Some examples of how knowledge design can improve user experiences include:

- Searching for "dry hair" on Lush.com in 2022 resulted in a list of every hair product Lush makes. The same search in 2023 delivered one result for "dry shampoo." Neither of these approaches utilizes knowledge design, which would focus on helping users solve a dry hair problem. Many users visit the site looking for solutions to various hair and beauty problems. The site should be searchable by common hair and skin issues, not just by products, smells, or moods.

- Many clothing retailers and manufacturers list their clothes by size, but most people know that brand sizes differ. It would be helpful if fitting information were collected from users, who could state that brand X fits similar to brands A, C, and G. For example, crowdsourced information informing visitors that one popular brand of blue jeans (brand W) has a tighter waist than another popular brand (brand L) of the same size, or a lesser-known brand J fits like popular brand C.

- The previously mentioned U.S. income tax software, TurboTax, is known for providing a wizard-style UI to guide users through the otherwise complicated task of calculating income tax. The wizard leads users to a successful result by dynamically adjusting the data input fields based on responses the users provide at the beginning of the task, e.g., single vs. married, W2 vs. self-employed or owner of a business, etc. Instead of facing a daunting, long, and complex form, this approach shields users from irrelevant and confusing options.

What Is a Knowledge Company?

It's easy to imagine a meeting where our teammates pat themselves on the back and declare that "we know our users and what they want." This is usually a display of inaccurate data, false confidence, and a bias that can lead teams to assume that research isn't necessary or important. Any company that provides a website, service, or product is much more knowledgeable about their domain than their individual users. But the idea of your company having more knowledge than your users is not a license to jump to conclusions or guess what users need.

Knowledge, not technology, is the core component of a successful design effort. The user knowledge profiles describe the knowledge that the users are likely to have when starting their task. Your users have only a basic set of knowledge about their task but will need additional knowledge to successfully complete that task. The difference between the knowledge users have and the knowledge they need is the **knowledge gap** that must be bridged by the design.

This is the opportunity for the company to impart their knowledge of the domain into the design, instead of relying on the users to somehow pick up that missing knowledge or get by without it. It is up to the company to bridge that knowledge gap.

Every knowledge opportunity is different based on the problem and the knowledge gap. The key to design success is to first identify the knowledge gap and *then* identify what knowledge the company has that can be embedded into the product to bridge that gap. Sometimes the company doesn't have that necessary knowledge, but ideally it should have the ability to realize this intelligence deficiency, know how to find it, and then inject it into the design. This is what makes a company a knowledge company.

Think back to the ProFlowers case study: they became the market leader of the online florist domain by using their knowledge of flowers and bouquets to organize their site around the occasion rather than the flowers. The research clearly showed that users wanted the right bouquet for their occasion, but they didn't know enough about flowers to build a bouquet, something the competitor florist websites expected their customers to do.

By organizing the bouquets into occasion categories, ProFlowers relied on the one piece of information users would know: the occasion. ProFlowers could then use their domain knowledge of flowers to organize the bouquets into occasions, making ProFlowers a knowledge company, not a flower company.

Apple Is a Knowledge Company

It has been said many times that, "Apple doesn't invent new technology; they just redesign it." Their storied success isn't just from creating pretty designs; it's from helping users succeed beyond their own capabilities. Apple succeeds by using their knowledge about user behaviors to create products that are much easier to use.

This means that Apple isn't just a product company; it's a knowledge company. User skills and knowledge are highly variable. Any design that relies on individual skill and knowledge can only succeed at a rate equally as variable as their users. Apple embeds their best practice knowledge into their products to avoid relying solely on their users' knowledge.

For example, in the mid-2000s, there were a dozen popular MP3 players on the market, and all were enjoying only a modicum of success. These were physical devices that stored and played MP3 audio files. Despite the coolness factor of the technology at the time, these machines didn't see more adoption because of the difficulty in using the technology.

Back in the day, there were 4 main steps to using an MP3 player:

1. Go to MP3.com or some other source, find some music, and download it onto your computer. It had to be in the MP3 format. Most players couldn't handle WAV, AIFF, or other formats.

2. Use a playlist manager such as MusicMatch® or WinAmp® to create playlists of your tracks.

3. Upload the playlist and music files to the device using its proprietary UI. Some players had no UI and expected you to connect the device like an external hard drive, and copy your files through Explorer ®or Apple Finder®.

4. Play the music loaded onto your device.

This process required at least four separate interfaces and was rather cumbersome for the non-tech-savvy user.

Apple didn't invent digital music and was a late entry into that domain. The original iPod® models didn't support digital music tasks well, nor were the devices themselves the true genesis of Apple's rebirth. Apple's meteoric success came not just from the iPod, but from the integration of the Apple Store® with iTunes®.

This integration didn't merely add a new product to the domain; it changed the paradigm so that all users could accomplish tasks easily. With the Apple Store and iTunes integration, the iPod reduced the number of interfaces and the number of steps to:

1. Go to iTunes to find and select some music. iTunes automatically downloads selected music to your iPod while it charges, with no user action required. Generic playlists by artist, album, genre, and decade are automatically created, with no user action required.

2. Play the music with the then-cool iPod jog dial interface.

This basically reduced the process from four user interaction steps and four interfaces to the "find and select music" step and only two interfaces.

Great UX is invisible, and this is one example. Unlike other MP3 players, this design did not require advanced technical knowledge. It did most of the work for the users, such as automatically downloading the music to their computer, automatically uploading it into the iPod, and auto-creating playlists.

Apple utilized their knowledge of user behaviors around digital music and optimized the task flow to reduce the dependency on individual user skill and knowledge. They injected their knowledge into the design to make it easier for users to succeed beyond their own capabilities.

Not a Knowledge-Oriented Design

An example of a company failing to leverage their knowledge to aid the user is demonstrated on the CustomInk.com website, as Debbie Levitt and I observed during a 2021 project for a competitor. Imagine a softball coach who wants a set of custom shirts for the team, including players' names and numbers. The 2021 process on Custom Ink had the following steps (and possible outcome):

1. Select a shirt style.

2. Choose a shirt color.

3. Create and upload their team logo.

4. Enter player names and numbers for the jerseys.

5. Find out at the very end that the selected shirt or color doesn't come in the sizes they need.

6. Start over, changing the selections to see if the required sizes are available in a different shirt or color.

Imagine how frustrating it is to put in all of that work and go through all of those steps, only to discover at the very end that the desired colors are not available in the desired sizes. How many sales were lost because of that user experience?

A better design might ask at the beginning of the process which colors, sizes, and quantities in each size the team needs, and the date by which the coach needs all of the shirts in hand. The system can then suggest only the shirt styles that will be in stock and able to be produced and shipped in time for the "needs by" date. The system can also suggest expedited production and/or shipping given the "needs by" date rather than leaving the coach to guess the correct options required to meet their deadline.

A better approach might be to provide a system that asks about:

1. The required sizes

2. The purpose of the product (sports, work, etc.)

3. The product type (shirt, shorts, socks, etc.)

4. The product specifics (short sleeve, long sleeve, etc.)

And then provide the user with a set of applicable options.

Knowledge Example: FedEx Print

What would you like to print today?

Upload Your File
Don't see what you're looking for?
Set custom printing options.

Flyers
Flyers make your announcements and events stand out from the competition.

Presentations
Show you mean business with professional presentation documents.

Posters
Posters are versatile communication tools that grab attention.

Poster with Mounting, Laminating
Poster packages include photo quality print mounted on rigid board and lamination.

Manuals in Binders
Manuals organize a lot of information in a manageable and engaging format.

Figure 47: The FedEx Print® web app landing page offering choices for common print job types, such as flyers, presentations, manuals in binders and more.

FedEx is a global courier and package delivery service that in 2004 bought Kinko's, a chain of American stores where you could copy documents or have professional printing jobs done. These stores are now called, "FedEx Office®."

My project with FedEx in the mid-2000s began with generative observational research to accurately define the problem. This included several FedEx representatives participating in the user observations as Subject Matter Experts to help identify key insights.

The team visited over a dozen FedEx print stores that were representative of typical operations at different times of the day, and observed:

- People requesting various kinds of print jobs.

- Clerks capturing the print order.

- Technicians creating the print jobs.

- Customers receiving and reviewing their completed print job.

These observations identified insights about the unmet user needs, which in turn drove a very successful design effort. After developing some interaction design mockups, users were invited to participate in evaluative research methods—specifically usability testing—to refine the designs. As expected, usability testing identified several key improvements.

Now let's walk through this story in slow motion.

Business Objective

FedEx needed an application successful enough to allow them to move the inefficient and inconsistent Kinko's Print Store printing operations to a more efficient centralized print location. Goals included reducing costs and increasing output quality. FedEx had tried a step-by-step wizard approach for users to define their printing jobs, which had failed.

Target User Knowledge Profile: Customers with complex printing projects

While some users merely needed to copy a page or two, or print a handful of copies of a document, the proliferation of cost-effective personal copiers and printers was eroding this revenue stream. FedEx needed to address the more complex print jobs that could not be completed with a personal printer. These jobs included specialized artifacts such as covers, tabs, and bindings.

The average print job requestor knew very little about how to define a print order well enough to meet their desired outcome. In many cases, it was observed that when people picked up their print job at the store, they often complained that it was not right. This was due to either the store clerk not understanding the user's request, or the requestor not knowing how to accurately describe their preferences or needs. In either case, it was paramount that the requestor be able to define their order accurately the first time.

One common target user for this type of online print tool was the traveling salesperson, who needed 30 copies of a proposal for a meeting in Chicago, followed by 20 copies the next day in Detroit. They did not want to carry these bulky documents on the plane but needed them in different places at specific times. The sales reps were too busy traveling to go to print shops in Chicago and Detroit and have them printed up in time for their meetings, nor could they take the chance of something going wrong with the print order at the print shop.

- **Trigger.** Needs copies of the proposal in different cities on different days.

- **Desired outcomes.** Impress the clients. Win the project. No mistakes.

- **Common knowledge.** Target users could be expected to know very little about complex print job options. They are more likely to recognize what they want once they see it. They have seen other print jobs and have some idea of what is possible. They have seen a bad print job before and want to avoid that kind of embarrassment.

- **Required knowledge.** The target user needs to have a conceptual idea about the end result of the print job. They need to be familiar with the various print product options.

Research Insights

The following specific insights were derived from the observational research and usability testing, and helped achieve an extraordinary and sustainable conversion rate.

- **UX design strategy.** The user research clearly and accurately redefined the problem: customers were focused on the appearance quality and presentation of the print job such as the bindings, tabs, and coversheet more than they were of the actual contents such as the report, spreadsheet, or training materials to be printed. The users had already finished creating the content elements and were now focused on how it all looked when put together.

  o FedEx's original strategy was a business-oriented strategy to reduce print job costs by standardizing the print process. Before FedEx acquired Kinko's, its print jobs were all customized, which was not very profitable. FedEx felt that standardizing the print process would reduce costs.

  o Our research clearly indicated that users wanted to know that their print job would turn out just like they imagined it. They wanted to visualize their print job, and then have it printed exactly that way.

  o The successful problem statement became, "Users need to have a clear expectation of the result of the print job *before* it is printed."

  o The UX strategy became, "Help the user visualize a quality print job to meet their expectations." The design solution was to create an image of the print job on screen and let users make changes.

- **Emotional investment.** Uploading their content and selecting a template initiated a personalized print job that users wanted to complete. Usability testing showed that users were genuinely interested and even happy to create something. They were more engaged than simply printing out a document. They tried different configurations out of interest and curiosity.

- **Baby steps.** A key aspect of our interaction design was to allow users to create print jobs over multiple sessions, allowing them to interrupt their project and pick up where they left off later. This was in stark contrast to the expectations inherent in visiting a brick-and-mortar store, where users felt compelled to define all of their print job options within that visit to the store. They did not want to make several trips to the store for one print job.

o   The ability to stop and restart a project helped ease users' fears of creating an imperfect print job. The print job itself was broken up into several steps that could be completed as needed. Moreover, other than supplying the actual content, there were no "required" steps to complete. The print job was always in a ready-to-print state.

- **Knowledge design.** By making everything visually oriented and displaying a representation of the expected result, users were much more successful in creating a print product that met their desired expectations. Common templates provided reasonable starting points for many users. Usage data confirmed that new customers tended to start with these templates and modified them to suit their needs. Some customers used their previous print jobs as templates.

  o   The resulting design leveraged this developed knowledge and suggested appropriate templates to each user.

  o   The users were provided with additional options, if desired, to make the print job creation more flexible. However, live usage data suggested that many users applied the best practice templates with few, if any, changes.

Outcome

The new design successfully brought a highly streamlined and profitable application to a lackluster brick-and-mortar operation. This increased profits far above projections and allowed FedEx to completely achieve their strategic objectives. Moreover, this new design has been in place for over 15 years and still performs well.

The new design offered some very well-designed templates representing the most common types of print jobs. These templates were derived from thousands of customer print job requests and reviewed by subject matter experts.

The users are not required to know anything about print jobs or the best design ideas for their job. They only need to know the purpose or function of the printouts, such as to conduct a workshop, to give a sales pitch, or offer a conference brochure. The rest of the process is supported by the knowledge built into the design.

Knowledge Design Approaches

Embedding the company's knowledge into the design reduces the reliance on user skill and knowledge, helping users succeed beyond their current capacity. Knowledge is more valuable than any other design element. It's what keeps users coming back to your solution. It's more than just a user interface. It sets your design apart from the competition, who can't easily copy your solution.

Instructions, training, help, and workarounds are not the solution. They are symptoms of design issues. These Band-Aids are an indication that a design does not meet user expectations or fit the user's understanding of their task very well. A good task-oriented knowledge-designed product will not require any of these Band-Aids.

You can avoid relying on instructions, training, or help as a design solution by applying any of these following design approaches:

- **Show an example**. A single example helps the user avoid guessing which action, information, or entry format is required. Showing a generic phone number as an example successfully informs the user without having to provide any instructions. Though helpful, examples are limited and tend to mostly indicate the format or type of input. They are static and do not change.

> +1 800-555-1212

+1 800-555-1212

Figure 48: Two different examples of a phone number format suggestion. One is hint text inside the field, which will disappear once the user types. They might forget the correct format once the model disappears. The second shows the correct phone number format above the field.

- o Note: While showing a model for the correct way to enter data such as phone numbers and dates can lead to more users entering these correctly, the real solution would be to have the system do the work. For example, for a ten-digit North American phone number, validate the field for ten numbers. If those are all there, then the system can handle changing or removing dashes, spaces, dots, parentheses, or other characters. The true upgrade in a case like this is to remove the cognitive demands and make any valid ten-digit phone number acceptable.

- **Provide templates**. A template is an example or model with many different attributes contained within it. For more complex knowledge requirements, a contextually relevant template avoids some user guesswork about which kinds of actions are required. This is especially true when each task demands varied or different inputs. Templates provide a curated example of what the system needs from the user for each task, eliminating the need for the users to know all of the types of inputs or actions that are required.

- o For example, if the user is trying to create custom printed T-shirts for a company event, the printing templates may differ based on the type of shirt selected. A T-shirt template might indicate where the image designs could go on the front and back. A corporate polo shirt template might only allow a logo on the left chest area and a line of text on the sleeve.

o   Templates are one of the easier ways to embed company knowledge into a design. Provide reasonable templates that are based on common user needs, such as frequent forms or fields.

o   A template is typically provided by the company based on some selection or action from the user. When the user selects a type of product on a website, they might be presented with a template of the type of information required for that product. The website might offer a set of fields for the user to indicate power requirements for a tool, such as North American or European power plug and voltage options, which are preselected based on the delivery address. Templates tend to be only partially dynamic.

o   A good template will address a large percentage of the intended audience. Templates may evolve over time as more data is collected.

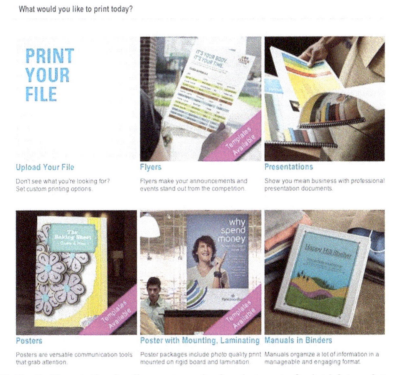

Figure 49: The FedEx printing landing page again showing a set of print job templates different print job types, such as presentations or training manuals in binders.

•   **Apply intelligent defaults**. When requesting user inputs, it is often more successful to include a common, valid answer. An intelligent default is more dynamic since it applies some knowledge of the users' situation and inserts likely answers or information.

o   For example, a common intelligent default is to utilize the user's known location to prefill the common address fields. Alternatively, a user could enter their postal code, and the system enters their city or town and state or province.

o   Google applies an intelligent default by "sniffing" the user's location to find things that are "near them." Another example of an intelligent default is to automatically select the most relevant choice based on previous entries or selections. For example, if a flower buyer selects flowers from the "birthday" category, offer them a birthday-themed note card to accompany the flowers.

o   Another less common approach is to combine reasonable choices together, such as pre-configured laptops that most brands offer. These make sense to most buyers, and few will need to change any of the choices, though editing a choice is only one click away.

o   Intelligent defaults differ from templates in that an intelligent default may be curated from data from usage behaviors of many users (common inputs to a field), but a template is based on the knowledge the company has about the problem.

o   Another example of an intelligent default is to reuse information about the user that they have already applied. For example, when filling out government forms, you may be asked several times for the same information. Why can't the system remember the repeated information and automagically populate the repeated fields?

- **Capture and apply crowdsourced data**. Capture commonly applied inputs or choices and use them to create an intelligent default. Google does this with search suggestions; as the user types in the search entry field, Google displays suggestions based on common searches others have executed.

o   Designers will not know in advance which data will be displayed since it is sourced from aggregate inputs of previous users that can change over time. The designers can only design for where the data goes, not for what the data will be.

o   The value of this data is that it evolves over time yet remains relevant. An example of this might be to provide a crowdsourced detail about a childcare center captured from social media comments, such as many users reporting that the childcare center is often too busy before 10:00 to answer questions over the phone. The crowdsourced data might be "Call the center after 10:00 a.m. They are too busy to answer questions before then."

o   This approach requires that the system include some way to capture this data from the users, such as including a review or user comments section in the interface. Also, be sure to maintain anonymity of the information sources by aggregating the data from these review or comment fields. Also be aware of any privacy issues in your region. In the USA, aggregated data can be used as long as individual identities cannot be derived from the data.

- **Create a best-practices task approach**. A designer who observes 100 users performing the same task 100 different ways might design an interface flexible enough to allow users to perform the task any way they want. The failed assumption here is that all of the users know what they are doing and how to do it well, and that it's best if we let everybody create a varied experience.

  o A great UX designer who sees 100 users doing the same task 100 different ways recognizes that there likely aren't 100 right ways to perform the task and that few users know how to perform the task *correctly or well*. The UX researcher has the ability to see beyond the users' four walls of their office— or current environment limitations—and learn what works well from many other users. Rather than designing a flexible site, consider designing a site that promotes a single *best-practices* path.

  o One noted difficulty with this best-practices approach is deciding when a single best-practice approach is the right solution, such as the iPod design approach, versus providing a flexible approach to the task, such as the FedEx print approach. Even when the design promotes a single best-practice approach, it could still allow for some flexibility by providing additional interface elements one click away.

  o For example, the user may want more control over a best-practice selection and click to open another screen offering more detailed selections or inputs. Best practices will never work for 100% of the users, but if the approach helps 80%-90%, then it succeeds beyond the overly flexible approaches quite well.

Invisibly Sharing Knowledge

If a design requires users to pay close attention to the interface to catch all of the details, there's something wrong with it. An interface should be invisible, rather than demand attention. It should not rely on the user to find stuff but should automatically present interaction cues to the user when relevant.

Consider the common door example that Don Norman popularized in his book, *The Design of Everyday Things*. As you are leaving the office building, you approach the door, instinctively grab the handle, and pull it because that's what you instinctively do with handles. To your shock and dismay, the door doesn't open. Then you see the little sign above the handle that says, "Push." You feel less than brilliant because you can't open something as simple as a door.

The design of that door interrupts the users' task, and conflicts with their mental model, resulting in a negative experience. If something as simple as a door requires instructions or user attention, there's something inherently wrong with the design. A door should not require users to pay special attention to it to use it correctly: it should not require instructions, tutorials, or training.

A flat panel on the door automatically invites only one action—the correct one—to push the door open. No attention is required. The flat panel is an "invisible" design because the user isn't required to give it any thought, nor does it interrupt the user. They probably don't even remember opening that door. That interface is invisible.

The more knowledge you can embed into the design to do more of the work for the user, the more invisible your design becomes. In the ProFlowers example, organizing the flowers by occasion eliminates the need for the user to pick specific flowers, they just select an occasion and see flowers appropriate for that occasion, without real effort on their part. Once they select a bouquet, they are guided through the checkout sequence, instead of a cumbersome shopping cart experience. Again, much more invisible.

Chapter 11: The Data-to-Action Sequence

Dashboards are a common design element in enterprise software, yet they are rarely done well. The point of a dashboard is to help the user identify an anomaly or trend, and take appropriate actions. Therefore, a dashboard needs to provide more than just data; it has to provide actionable insights.

Think of a dashboard as providing knowledge along a sequence that ranges from data to action. The best dashboards drive users to perform the right actions that achieve a desired outcome. A dashboard that leaves users to figure out what to do next is just a pretty picture.

The range of knowledge consists of the following:

Data ⟶ Information ⟶ Insight ⟶ Action

Figure 50: The Data-to-Action Sequence: data to information to insight, to action.

Data is simply a number. This is the least actionable end of the sequence. Data alone does not suggest any action. For example, a dashboard might show the number 95, but what does that tell the user to do? At the data level, we are completely dependent upon individuals' highly variable skills. As was mentioned before, any design that relies on individual levels of skill and knowledge cannot succeed at a rate any greater than the highly variable skills of the users.

Information is data with context, such as relatedness or scale. This provides a little more help for the user, but still cannot drive a specific behavior that will identify and correct an issue. Most dashboard displays are still dependent on user skill to determine which actions to take.

For example, a dashboard might display that your conversion rate tracks at 12% in step three of a seven-step conversion funnel. That doesn't suggest any specific action to improve that conversion rate. Moreover, it doesn't even indicate if it's a problem. Maybe 12% is acceptable or even good. But how would the user know?

To continue our earlier example, if the dashboard showed the number 95, and we now have context telling it that it represents degrees Fahrenheit, what does it indicate? A warm day? Hot? Is this good or bad? What action does it suggest? None.

Insight is produced by including additional information to help identify that something is tracking normally or abnormally. This might include forecasts based on current trends, industry averages, etc. This moves the user closer to an actionable state, but still relies on the aforementioned highly variable individual skills. Applying insights drives the design towards solving a real problem and suggests a specific action. This is where innovation emerges.

For example, if the dashboard displays user abandonment rates along the conversion flow, how do designers know if those rates are a problem? Consider adding lines that compare the conversion rates to a target or to industry averages to determine whether they are exceptional or acceptable. A dashboard could even compare a previous design to a new one to determine if the new design were more effective (or not), and by how much. Identify thresholds of good and bad values, and indicate that a metric has crossed a threshold.

For example, chicken should be cooked to 165 degrees Fahrenheit. The chicken in the oven is only 95 degrees. What was previously considered a warm day (95 degrees) is now raw chicken. We will need to cook the chicken more. Do we need more time? Higher temperatures? The dashboard still lacks an actionable step.

Action is about the real goal of any data analysis: identify a problem and affect a solution. Charts and graphs provide static information, but don't suggest corrective actions. This end of the sequence requires more work to design, but ultimately results in a dashboard that drives appropriate user behaviors. Part of the design effort includes analyzing potential problems and identifying actions that correct them. Find a way to define and embed actionable knowledge into the design.

Wrapping up our example, we would want to send a clear message to cook the chicken at 375 degrees for 20 more minutes to reach the appropriate 165 degree serving temperature. This is an action that achieves the desired outcome.

Why Dashboards Suck

Pretty much every dashboard fails to serve its most basic and primary function, which is to identify problems and help correct them. It's rare for a dashboard to inform users about where a problem is or what to do about it. Most dashboards show little more than static, non-actionable information in pretty colors. They're nothing more than shiny objects.

A key tenet of UX design is that every element should drive a specific and desired behavior. What actions do most dashboards suggest? None. "Drilling down into the data" might not help the user recognize or solve a problem. Exporting the data means that what people really need to do can't be done in the dashboard; their real work is not supported by the dashboard. These dashboards rely on the users to do all of the work to determine which actions to take.

A good dashboard should do three things:

- Identify trends.

- Highlight exceptions or anomalies.

- Drive appropriate actions that solve a problem.

Here's a common type of dashboard graph depicting sales performance:

Figure 51: A typical dashboard showing static sales information. Various bars are various colors and heights for six sales reps.

How well does this dashboard answer the following basic questions:

- What's the problem?

- What's the cause of the problem?

- What can be done about it?

- Which action does this suggest or drive?

Dashboards are typically a manifestation or visualization of the existing data. *We have data; let's display it!* A better approach is to start with the desired outcome, such as conversion funnel performance and potential improvements, and then work backwards toward determining which data is required to create a visualization that promotes the right actions.

Since trends or exceptions are key indicators that drive appropriate actions, the system needs to "understand" what constitutes anomalous trends or data. One approach includes defining thresholds. When a data point crosses a threshold, it is deemed exceptional. There's usually a logical reason why it's a definable threshold, and it usually relates to a potential corrective action.

This approach:

1. Determines which goals you are trying to achieve.

2. Identifies which indicators you want to see regarding those goals.

3. Defines the thresholds that dictate an exception.

4. Determines which actions you would take to correct the exception.

Of course, this is a simplified version of the process. It's more common to find that you don't have all of the information in the existing data set to create a truly actionable dashboard; then you have to build ways of collecting the data that really matters before building your dashboard. The end result is a true problem-solving tool rather than just some simple eye-candy.

Example: Actionable Visualization

Here is a wireframe of a Vanguard investment dashboard design concept that drives a specific action. In this case, the user has too many shares of tech stocks across their four different portfolios (retirement, college, vacation cabin, and classic car hobby). The system is suggesting a specific action, to sell some stocks. That resolves the issue, transforming static data into something that drives an appropriate action.

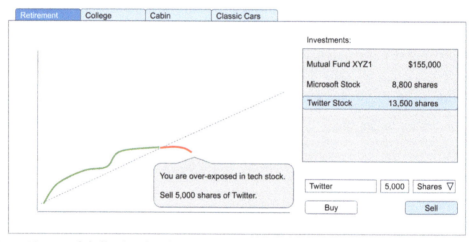

Figure 52: A graph indicating that the investment is trending below the objective and a suggested action to correct it.

Case Study: A Data-to-Action Dashboard

One of my projects involved creating a dashboard for pharmaceutical sales reps. The original design was not even a dashboard, but pages and pages of numbers and data. It wasn't helping the reps sell any better, mostly because sales reps would rather meet with customers than analyze reams of data.

The goal of each rep was to meet their sales quotas in order to make their bonuses. Tracking sales forecasts towards a target metric indicated whether or not they were going to make their bonus that year. The company had developed sales formulas that could reliably predict sales performance based on the number of customer visits for each customer. Some customers required more visits, while others required fewer visits. By tracking the sales reps' customer visit frequency, the formula could suggest that the rep visit specific customers more frequently.

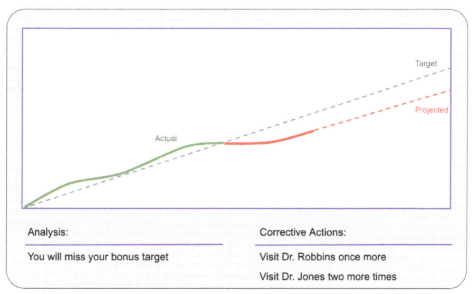

Figure 53: Sales performance dashboard with suggested actions.

Pages of useless data requiring hours of analysis were replaced with a formula-based forecasting design that took only seconds to indicate anomalies and their corrective actions. This dashboard design remains the industry standard for the pharmaceutical sales domain.

What if the dashboard instead identified which steps in the sales process people were performing poorly? What if it suggested that people were setting appointments during the customers' busiest time of the day or week or month? What if it suggested a visitation schedule that was more conducive to the customer's schedule? This approach would indicate that the company needs to collect data about the busy and free times for their customers in order to improve the success of the sales team.

Rather than merely displaying data that the company already has, use UCD research processes and the Data-to-Action Sequence to identify data that is required but missing. Such a design would include identifying which data the company needs to collect as well as how to display it.

Knowledge design applies to more than just simple dashboards and websites, and can solve rather complex problems. The following describes a very complex problem that illustrates how Artificial Intelligence (AI) fits into the knowledge-oriented design approach.

Chapter 12: Case Study: Artificial Intelligence as Knowledge

Aircraft and pilot scheduling in the Air Force usually takes two people about a week to complete. It typically requires immense effort to develop a complex schedule that meets all the training objectives and priorities. Last-minute rescheduling is even more difficult, resulting in scrubbed missions or missed training. Schedulers use a myriad of tools and processes to solve this problem such as disjointed apps, puck boards (a type of whiteboard), and spreadsheets.

Ultimately, the complex scheduling task is performed in the heads of humans, not in scheduling "tools." These are not really scheduling tools, just *schedule-capture tools*. Rather than creating a schedule, these tools only provide a way for the user to represent or share a schedule created in their head. A lack of standardization across different squadrons and units means every scheduling process is different, resulting in a steeper learning curve when aircrews transfer to new units, and making it difficult for schedulers to assist sister squadrons.

Now imagine a day when a squadron's flight scheduler arrives at the office and creates the next week's flight schedule before their coffee gets cold. If one of the pilots scheduled for tonight's inflight refueling exercise calls in sick, the scheduler marks the pilot as "unavailable," and the system recalculates and schedules another pilot who needs night refueling practice. Total time on task: five minutes. Here is that story.

Artificial Intelligence/Machine Learning to the Rescue

The user experience team conducted observational user research at several squadrons. They discovered that units typically have the same scheduling problems but solve them differently with custom solutions, custom apps, and custom spreadsheets. The biggest issue was that regardless of the tools used, the process placed high demands on user cognition, thus relegating each solution to the limitations of each individual scheduler's capabilities and processes.

A solution to this problem relies on reducing the demands on human cognition by developing a system that balances complex needs and priorities to create a workable schedule. From the research, my UX team defined a single, enterprise-wide Smart Scheduler Paradigm that can be applied to various scheduling tasks across the Air Force such as pilot scheduling, Airman training, and readiness forecasting/preparation.

The Smart Scheduler Paradigm is an Artificial Intelligence (AI)/Machine Learning (ML) algorithm designed to do the work for humans, effectively reducing the cognitive burden of balancing varying assets (planes, classrooms, bomb ranges, etc.) and personnel needs (vacation, dental appointments, etc.).

After a system is primed with rules-based objectives, assets or resources, personnel, and adjustable parameters and priorities, the system is designed to automatically generate a suggested schedule. Users can then adjust the parameters, such as indicating a pilot is out sick or that a plane is down for maintenance, which would trigger the system to recalculate the schedule. This Smart Scheduler Paradigm will reduce the typical pilot scheduling efforts from around 60 hours per week to roughly 30 minutes. Other scheduling tasks will likely see similar benefits.

Smart Scheduler Paradigm

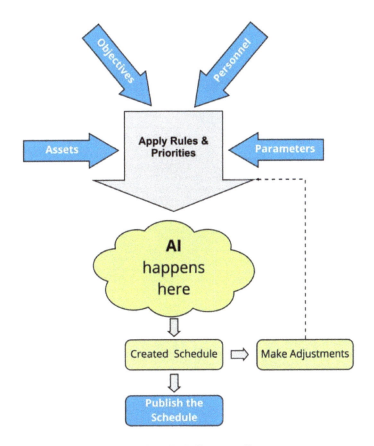

Figure 54: The scheduling paradigm.

The Smart Scheduler task flow is quite simple, only requiring that users define the different elements of the system, objectives, and priorities one time. The system is ready to calculate a new schedule with each new parameter adjustment.

Smart Scheduler Task Flow

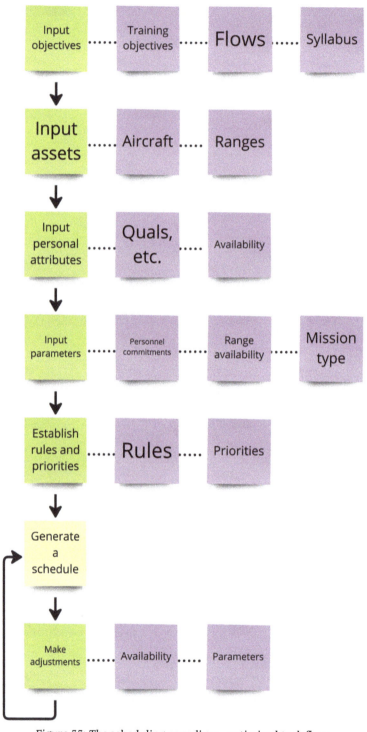

Figure 55: The scheduling paradigm - optimized task flow.

Scheduling Paradigm Flow, Optimized:

- **User:** Input objectives. **Artifact:** Training objectives, Flows, Syllabus.

- **User:** Input assets. **Artifact:** Aircraft, Ranges.

- **User:** Input personal attributes. **Artifact:** Quals, etc., Availability.

- **User:** Input parameters. **Artifact:** Personnel commitments, Range availability, Mission type.

- **User:** Establish rules and priorities. **Artifact:** Rules, Priorities.

- **System:** Generate a schedule.

- **User:** Make adjustments. **Artifact:** Availability, Parameters.

- Cycle by going back to **System:** Generate a schedule.

Institutional Knowledge and Best Practices

A key benefit of a common design paradigm is that it captures best practices from shared institutional knowledge across the enterprise rather than the disparate knowledge specific to individual solutions. This sharing of a common knowledge approach drives systemic improvement and efficiency gains rather than incremental improvements at the unit level.

In other words, this paradigm fits all scheduling tasks rather than creating one-off solutions for each scheduling problem, and helps promote a single best-practice approach.

This case study highlights how UX research identified and redefined the problem, thus enabling an accurate characterization for an AI/ML algorithm that represented the knowledge to inject into the product. The knowledge design process identified ways to create a system that does more of the actual scheduling work for the user rather than just creating another schedule capture tool.

Chapter 13: Example Travel Project: Knowledge Design

Remember Pat? Pat needs to travel from LA to NYC, and has a lot of limitations and needs. We previously looked at their task analysis, optimized task flow, knowledge profile, and mental model. What is the **knowledge design opportunity** for people like Pat?

Pat has never been to New York City and does not know how to get around the area. This includes determining which airport to fly into or which mode of transportation to use to get from the airport to the hotel, especially at rush hour. These options change dramatically depending on the flight arrival time or which airport is used.

The opportunity here is to determine how to capture that local transportation knowledge and apply it so that it supports Pat's mental model of a **digital travel agent**. For example, a travel agent would know to use the subway during rush hour instead of buses or cars. The solution might require designing a mechanism to capture this local knowledge, such as analyzing traffic patterns and travel times, and identifying crowd-sourced information that users leave in review sites.

Good designs require more than just an interface; they rely on the system performing some analysis or calculations that users might otherwise have to perform in their heads, such as figuring out how long it will take to get from the airport to the hotel, and using that information to figure out which flight to take. Such analysis or calculations represent the knowledge that can be embedded in the design to help the users succeed beyond their own skills and knowledge.

Our knowledge-oriented system works backwards to make the best recommendations for Pat. Pat needs to be at a 7:00 p.m. dinner at Serendipity 3, a restaurant at 225 E. 60th St., New York, NY 10022. Pat's profile in our system shows that they marked themselves as unfamiliar with NYC.

Through public data or APIs like Google Maps® and flight booking systems, our system can know that:

Figure 56: Map of the New York City area showing the 3 main airports relative to Manhattan.

- New York's LaGuardia Airport is closest to the destination, but would require Pat to take a bus, which will be ugly at rush hour.

- Even though it is in New Jersey, Newark Airport is close enough to be a viable option, but requires taking a train to New York City and making a cumbersome transfer to the subway to get to midtown.

- JFK Airport is the best option. Pat can take a train from the airport and make an easy transfer at the Jamaica train station to the E subway. It should take only a few minutes to get from the Lexington and 53rd Street E subway station to the hotel. This trip might take about an hour in total.

- Pat would need to land no later than 5:30 p.m. Pat's profile indicates that they prefer nonstop flights. Pat doesn't want to risk a plane change that could disrupt their schedule.

- There are a handful of nonstop flights from LAX to JFK on American Airlines®, Delta Airlines®, and JetBlue® that arrive before 5:30 p.m. Our system can check which airlines still have first-class seats available and only present those options.

- Knowing Pat prefers to travel in style, and that they will have to get back to JFK the next day to fly home, the system suggests Concorde Hotel at 127 E. 55th St, just a few blocks from the restaurant, and close to the E subway station for the trip back to the airport.

- Our system offers Pat a few choices with clear timing and pricing. We show Pat how to get from the airport to the hotel and later to the restaurant. Our smartphone app can integrate Google Maps and Google's Augmented Reality "Live View" walking directions to keep Pat from making mistakes. We tell Pat how to use Apple Pay® or Google Wallet® to pay for the subway.

Our system is now truly the digital travel agent that matches Pat's needs and mental models. Pat wants someone to figure this out for them and give them a narrow set of specifically curated choices. A mountain of our green sticky note "user steps" can be replaced by entering in some of Pat's needs (7:00 p.m. dinner at Serendipity 3, and that they must travel from Los Angeles on the same day), and letting the system do the rest. Pat chooses their preferred itinerary, and our system books their flight and hotel.

If this system doesn't already exist, Larry and Debbie invented it while writing this book. It could be innovative and disruptive for travelers of many types. Debbie Levitt wishes she had a system like this when she tried to figure out how to be in her Denver, Colorado, hotel room by midnight when she was speaking the same day at 2:00 p.m. at a Nashville, Tennessee, conference.

Now that you've identified what kind of knowledge you can embed into a design, it's time to start designing. Rather than the typical feature-oriented approach, the next section describes how to design for the users' tasks, embedding knowledge to support the users' task. Again, this process utilizes the information derived from this step to perform the next step.

Getting More Buy-In for Knowledge Design

Use this opportunity to explain the design rationale, including descriptions of which company knowledge elements to embed in the design. Post a short explanation of the required knowledge and how you expect to collect and present that knowledge. This should be posted alongside the user knowledge profiles and task flows. Indicate how it addresses the knowledge gap for that profile and task.

Remind stakeholders that since knowledge-oriented designs are based on the knowledge within the company, this provides an inherent competitive advantage that cannot be duplicated or "borrowed" by the competition. Moreover, your design will be more recognizable than the competitors' designs.

PART 6: TASK-ORIENTED DESIGN

Chapter 14: Design to the Tasks

Now that you have defined the "requirements" in terms of task flow and user knowledge, and identified the higher priority tasks and overarching UX strategy, it's finally time to start designing.

People use your website, app, or system because they have a problem to solve. The product should resonate with that problem, and then guide the user down a path specifically designed to solve that problem.

The optimized task analysis clearly identifies what the user is trying to achieve and how they should accomplish it. Your remaining green sticky notes indicate which actions the user needs to take. The purple stickies suggest what the user will need in order to complete that step: a tool of some type, knowledge or information, a form, etc.

Additional content or features that don't directly support the specific task *increase* the cognitive burden. Users are forced to figure out what that extra feature does and how it relates to their goal. The assumption is that if it's there, it must be important, even if it turns out to be unnecessary. More is not better in this case.

For example, our system wouldn't ask Pat if they would like tickets to the museum or a Broadway show. We know Pat is flying in and out with no time for other activities. We don't try to upsell Pat on a rental car; we advised Pat to not get a car or use car or bus transportation when time is tight.

So Many Tools, So Little Knowledge

You just bought a used car, and need to change the spark plugs in the car's engine. Your buddy invites you to use his garage full of tools while he is away this weekend. To your surprise, he has a whole stack of professional tool chests with labels identifying the tools in each drawer: a drawer of screwdrivers, one for with sockets, another with wrenches, etc. Perfect!

Then you realize that—never having changed spark plugs before—you have no idea which tools you actually need. You are further confused as you start opening all the drawers and find more tools than you have ever seen before. You have no idea what some of these tools even do.

Undaunted, you grab a handle and socket, but the spark plug socket doesn't fit the handle. You grabbed a 1/2" drive handle and the socket uses a 3/8" drive. Who knew? You give up for now.

Although it contains all the tools you could ever need, this garage is highly dependent on the user knowing exactly which tools they need for each job, and how to best use those tools.

Figure 57: A toolbox drawer full of various socket wrenches and sockets.

Your UX designer friend also invited you to use her garage this weekend to change your spark plugs. She has a garage full of tool chests, too, but the drawers are labeled by the tasks you need to perform, such as "change tire" or "change oil."

You quickly spot a drawer labeled "change spark plug." You open it to find just the tools you need for that job: socket handle, spark plug socket, socket extension (for those plugs way in the back), torque wrench (preset to 15 lb/ft), and gap tool (you didn't even know you have to gap the plugs).

This task-oriented toolbox design only requires each user to know which job they want to perform, such as remove the old plug, gap the new plug, and insert the new plug, torquing it to a specific setting. (There are plenty of videos online to help with that task.) By using her knowledge of which tools are appropriate for each task, the UX designer provided a design based on her expert knowledge that overcomes the highly variable skill and knowledge levels of each user. Instead of opening all of the drawers to find the tools they need, the user only has to open one. By virtue of her "design," the designer dramatically increases the success rate for every user, even the most novice mechanic.

Not Enough Features for the Task

In early 2023, Debbie Levitt was investigating UX research video call tools that would allow her as the session moderator to give the participant a unique URL and observers a separate URL for the call. This would allow participants to see the moderator, but not the observers.

One system had no way to change your camera or microphone once the session started. Albeit rarely, Debbie has had her microphone suddenly fail, forcing her to switch to another. Debbie could easily envision a research session when her microphone goes haywire, and she can't tell the system to switch to a different one, eventually causing her to abruptly end the interview. The lack of this feature was a dealbreaker.

In another system, there was no call URL for the moderator, and no clear way for the moderator to join the call. Through a conversation with support, Debbie learned that she was supposed to join as an observer, but then claim the moderator spot (before another observer does, which is risky when you have teammates who would love to be the moderator). In the "give everybody the right URL for their involvement" task, this tool is missing features.

In both cases, teams likely decided that their products were "good enough," and they either hadn't considered these aspects of the task, or deemed them too low priority to build. This could be a prioritization mistake. However, it's more likely that without making the effort to understand and map common user tasks, these vendors didn't even know what they had forgotten.

Feature-Oriented vs. Task-Oriented Design

A feature-oriented design typically organizes various features and functions by their relationship or similarity to each other, such as File, Edit, and View. In the case of the toolboxes, the first toolbox was organized by the features (tools), not the tasks. Additionally, a feature-oriented design typically includes only one instance of each feature in the interface. Users must know where each feature is and when to use them. When users want to save a file, they must know to go into the File menu to find that feature.

Years ago, there were no buttons on the screens; interface designers put everything in menus (File, Edit, and so on). These menus depended on the users understanding how items were grouped together and learning where to look for things. The menus were organized by how the developers understood the features, not how the user needed them organized.

One well-known application had a menu labeled "User." It contained any feature that had the word "user" in the name. Organizing menus and features by arbitrary labels doesn't take a user's perspective into account. Users are more likely to expect the features to be organized by their functional attributes.

User research found evidence that menus have a steep learning curve. Contextual menus (right-click menus) offer a little more help to the users, but can still be somewhat clunky to use. Little has changed with menu-driven products.

Another aspect of feature-oriented sites or apps is the emphasis on bells and whistles, gimmicky features that don't help users achieve their tasks, that detract/distract users from their task, such as clicking on a button to alert your social network about what you just bought online. The novelty of these features may attract initial attention, but if there are other more serious defects with the site, conversions or engagement will be short-lived.

A task-oriented design organizes features within the various task flows. Instead of just one interface where the user has all of the features available, such as a word processor with all of the features organized in ribbon menus on top of the application, a task-oriented design creates a separate set of screens for each different task. Each feature is provided on just the right screen in an order that follows the optimized task flow.

Given that a feature might be used in several different tasks, a basic tenet of task-oriented design is that a feature will be replicated in each task flow that requires it. This eliminates relying on the users having to know where each feature is in an application or when exactly to use it.

One task-oriented approach common to word processors is that the software switches to a separate mode when users want to format the header or footer of a document. This mode limits the actions and artifacts available to the header and footer. We think of it as a quasi-task-oriented design because some aspects, such as page numbers, are organized as a set of features requiring specific knowledge to use correctly.

One common example of a useful task-oriented design approach is the use of context menus, or right-click menus. Rather than having to hunt through all of the ribbon menu choices at the top of a word processor application, the software provides a common set of features when the user right-clicks on content in the application. Only those features that apply to the selected content or task appear in the pop-up menu.

A key attribute specific only to task-oriented design is that you can build best-practice knowledge into such a design, whereas you cannot do that well in a feature-oriented design. A best practice for a task might move or eliminate features on specific screens, and each task would follow a specific task flow. Given that there might be several tasks, there might be several different flows. A feature-oriented design doesn't have different screens or flows for different tasks, so it cannot support a task-oriented approach.

The difficulty of creating a best-practice approach in a feature-oriented design is illustrated by the comparison of task-oriented meal-in-a-box products to traditional cooking practices. Each meal-in-a-box contains the exact ingredients in just the right quantities needed to cook that specific meal. When you open the box, you have just the right things to complete your task: task-oriented. Instead of a recipe, it just has a list of steps that result in a correctly prepared meal.

Your kitchen pantry represents the traditional feature-oriented approach; it contains a host of ingredients without focusing on any specific meal. Without a recipe, it's just a bunch of unrelated ingredients. If you find a recipe you like, there's no guarantee that you will have all of the ingredients or quantities for that recipe. Following a recipe also requires some level of cooking knowledge or confidence that many people don't seem to have (if the success of these task-oriented meal services is any indication).

Another analogy for task-oriented vs. feature-oriented designs is kitchen utensils and appliances. A hand peeler's shape provides obvious cues to how it should be used; it is fairly easy to learn how to successfully peel vegetables and even make chocolate shavings. In contrast, a food processor requires consulting the manual to figure out how to assemble all the components and correctly use the buttons for different food prep tasks. Many accessories are included with the machine and require considerable assembly and trial and error. Many of these are also not needed for frequent use and are put away in storage. These features can be overkill if the user only needs to slice carrot coins once in a while.

Key Element: One Task per Interface

A task-oriented approach focuses each screen or interface (menu, pop-up, etc.) on one and only one task, with the exception of the "starting" screen, where the user selects the task they want to perform. A task may require multiple screens, but each screen should be designed to support one specific task. This reduces the number of choices the user has to make at each step of a task, and avoids the confusion of determining which features belong to which task in a feature-oriented design approach.

Another important aspect of task-oriented design is identifying what to include and what to exclude from the design. To quote Antoine de Saint-Exupéry, "Perfection in design is achieved not when there is nothing left to add, but when there is nothing left to take away." Every element of a design should be there with a purpose that directly relates to the task at hand. Avoid those "wouldn't it be cool if..." design ideas.

Eliminating features or elements that do not directly support the current step of the specified task is a form of knowledge design. The designer should know which features support the current task better than the users will. As noted, additional features increase user confusion and the cognitive effort required to complete the task correctly. It forces the users to wonder why a feature is there and whether they should be using it. Limiting the design to just those features that directly support the current task makes it easier for the user to figure out what to do.

Task-Oriented Designs Look Different

A task-oriented design approach generates designs that look very different from almost every other design. If a new design looks pretty much like the current design or the competitor's design, the designers have failed. Even if the other company followed a task-oriented approach, they don't have the same knowledge that your company has to add into the design, which should make a noticeable difference in the resulting designs.

As an example, B2B websites typically follow the digital brochure model, where content is organized in a product- or service-oriented arrangement like a brochure or catalog. This arrangement reflects how the company sees itself as a provider of these products or services. Visitors are not yet familiar with the products and services, and all of their brand names. This design style relies on them reading and assimilating all of the information to determine what is relevant to their needs. This also relies on the users understanding enough about their problems to determine which solutions actually fit their needs.

A more successful approach is simply to list the most common problems on the home page (much like the occasions in the ProFlowers design), and then display more relevant information when the user selects a problem. This presents a screen that focuses on providing more information about the selected problem. Avoid adding content that doesn't directly relate to the selected problem. Additionally, if your product solves a number of problems, focus on the most common eight to ten (or fewer) to try to keep the interface streamlined and organized.

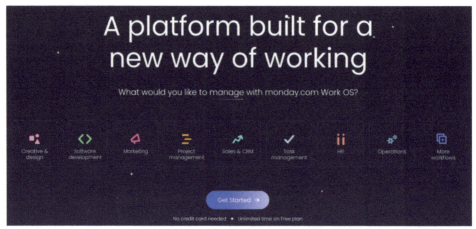

Figure 58: Monday.com's homepage in early 2023 offers eight clear paths including "marketing" and "project management," plus a "more workflows" option for people who don't immediately connect with any of the eight options.

Example: Kelley Blue Book

KBB.com in 2013 Had Four Calls to Action

KBB is the Kelley Blue Book, a website where people can determine the value of new and used cars. The 2013 version of the KBB.com homepage included four buttons. According to the KBB research and usage data, this confused the users.

Figure 59: An early version of the KBB homepage with four main call-to-action buttons: What should I pay for a new car, What should I pay for a used car, What's my current car worth, and Which car is right for me?

I had suggested using only two call-to-action buttons: pricing new and used cars (one button), and "What is my car worth?" KBB decided to create an additional button for "Which car is right for me?" and they split pricing new and used cars into two buttons, one for new cars and one for used cars.

KBB.com in 2016 Had Three Calls to Action

Given the user research results indicating that the four-buttons approach was not performing as well, the 2016 version reduced the choices to three buttons, but research and data indicated that the choices still confused the users. The user has not even identified what kind of car they want yet or what they should pay. The third call-to-action assumed that the user wants to see a list of cars for sale.

Figure 60: A 2016 version of the KBB.com homepage with only three main buttons: Price New/Used Cars, Check My Car's Value, and See Cars for Sale.

KBB.com in 2022 Had Two Main Calls to Action

The 2022 version of the homepage focused on the two main problems that users intend to solve with the website: determine what their car is worth or how much to pay for another car. There are other buttons, but it's obvious that the site focuses on those two main tasks.

Figure 61: A 2022 version of the KBB.com homepage highlighting only the two most important call-to-action buttons: Price New/Used, and My Car's Value.

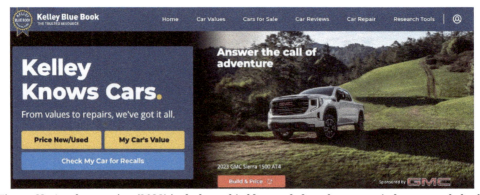

Figure 62: Another version (2023) includes a third button below the two main buttons to help the user check for recalls on their vehicle. Note that this third button is medium blue on dark blue, and designed to be less visible than the two main buttons.

This new third button allowing users to check for recalls creates a personally relevant reason for someone to return to this site, even if they aren't interested in selling their car or buying another one. This task includes a vehicle identification feature similar to the other two buttons, but is slightly different to support this new "Check My Car for Recalls" task.

Solve for the Entire Task

Feature-oriented designs focus on features rather than tasks, and consequently fail to support an entire task flow, the true end-to-end-journey. When conducting task observations, look beyond the immediate task and observe what happens before and after the task. Look beyond the time in which the user might be in your ecosystem (your site, your store, your products or services). What happens before the users start the task can have a profound effect on how they perceive the problem, and thus the solution as well.

The Full Arc of the Task

In 2020, Debbie Levitt and I researched how crafters and artists list items they want to sell online. We noted how much preparation they conduct prior to being in the marketplace's ecosystem (website) and listing the item for sale. The task isn't, "Take some photos and write a description paragraph." Creators stage the item, and take and edit numerous photos of the item. They research the details and features of the item, compare prices of similar items, and read similar ads for ideas of how to describe their item. They had tools and sneaky ways to try to figure out the best keywords and tags for their listing.

Once they publish their ad, some review it live on the site to ensure that it displays correctly. Some later reviewed analytics to understand why it wasn't selling well.

Rather than focusing on just the listing creation tasks, we identified additional opportunities by investigating the tasks that happened before and after the listing page. Among other actionable ideas, we suggested that the marketplace design a pricing calculator tool in the listing page to help sellers understand the best pricing for their item (based on the system's knowledge of how similar items sell) and to calculate their profit after listing and other fees (which were often unknown until the item sold). This would build in knowledge the selling platform has related to average pricing or what price might lead to more sales.

A design artifact common to enterprise domains is the ubiquitous scheduling app. Most designs tend to focus on the scheduling app when that is just an artifact of a greater task, a means to an end. Much like the Air Force scheduling example described previously, most designs rely on the user to perform the actual scheduling in their head, which means that the interface really only captures the schedule in the system rather than taking any work off of the user. Instead, think about what the desired end state of creating a schedule is, and design for that.

For example, one of my large projects was for a medical product design that focused on administering medications to patients according to their doctor's orders. Part of the task required the charge (or lead) nurse to assign nurses in the oncoming shift to patients. The original technology-oriented design approach was based on the assumption that it was a one-to-many problem, one nurse with many patients. Moreover, the design required the charge nurse to manually enter the schedule into the application.

The user research observations identified that the charge nurses took a different approach to nurse-patient assignments. Rather than being nurse-oriented, they used a patient-oriented perspective. An overriding driver of patient assignments was a focus on "continuity of care." This meant that they tried to assign the nurse who had the most recent familiarity with the selected patient. Rather than go down a list of nurses and randomly assign patients, the charge nurse would go down the list of patients and ask, "Who had that patient most recently?"

The resulting design approach was to make the system create an intelligent default starting schedule based on the data about which nurses were working that shift, who the patients were, and which nurse was the most recent caregiver for each patient. The charge nurse could adjust that schedule as needed, but it still reduced their workload and optimized the schedule to provide the best continuity of care.

The main objective of the assignment task went beyond assigning nurses to patients. It also drove the medication dispensing tasks for the nurses. This aligned the system with the patients, their medications, and the nurse responsible for those meds. This drove a design that ensured the system kept track of the meds for each patient, which was the primary goal of this product. The assignment was just a part of that greater task.

Ultimately, the system kept track of the various factors that influenced nursing assignments, and automatically generated suggested assignments, completely eliminating the need for a human to perform this assignment task.

Replicate Content and Features

An obvious indication that a site or application is *not* task-oriented is that each feature exists in just one place in the app or website. This feature-oriented design approach relies on the users knowing where each feature is, how and when to use it in their task, and also when *not* to use it. A more successful design organizes features by the task the user is performing, even if that means replicating a feature in multiple places.

For example, feature X might be used in several tasks. Since it is used in different steps of each task, the task flow for Task 1 might be features A, X, D, C, but for Task 2 the flow might be A, C, D, X, G. Rather than relying on the users to know in which order to use which features, the system would offer users several common tasks, and then provide the features in the right order for each selected task.

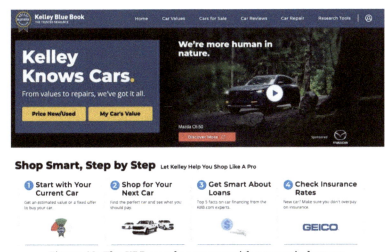

Figure 63: The KBB.com homepage with two main buttons.

The KBB.com website is a good example of this approach. The two task paths, *find out how much to pay for a car* (Price New/Used) or *determine the value of your car* (My Car's Value) utilize the same vehicle identification tool to specify the year, make, model, and options of a vehicle, but each task uses the vehicle selection tool slightly differently. Rather than expecting the user to know how to use the tool differently, the site presents different versions of the same feature that are optimized for the selected task.

When a seller wants to determine a reasonable selling price for their car, they know all of its specific details, such as mileage, trim package, whether it has a navigation system, etc. This information more accurately determines the value of the car.

When a user is trying to determine how much to pay for a car, they may have a model year, but will not know the actual mileage of any specific vehicle (yet), which trim options they will be looking at, and specific options a car may have. They will be looking for a general price range until they find a specific vehicle. The user will use the same tool, but the design presents it differently based on the different knowledge the user has for each of the two tasks.

Avoid "What If" Scenarios

A common mistake when designing is to postulate, "What if the user wanted to do X?" If that user wanted to do X, it would have been noticed in the observations or interviews and ended up as a critical path in the task analysis. Focus on the most common task scenarios, even if it means leaving out a task or step that isn't done frequently or at all.

Designing for these exceptions typically results in making the more common task cumbersome or difficult to do. This common design mistake is often the result of the business representatives being afraid to "leave money on the table." The theory is that you should solve every problem for every user, which ironically usually results in doing neither well. You cannot hope to solve for every user problem. This problem is similar to the "wouldn't it be cool if..." design idea problem.

Generating Emotional Investment

Although much has been written about using video and images to increase user attraction and engagement, these have limited success. There are more effective ways to emotionally engage with the user, such as providing a means for the users to make their interactions more *personally relevant*.

Create a design that gets the user to interact with the site or product to generate a meaningful, personally relevant artifact without requiring much commitment from the user. It doesn't need to be highly valuable, but it must be relevant. The effort the user expends to interact with that artifact creates an emotional investment that gives them a reason to return. User research typically uncovers at least one element that can be leveraged to create an emotionally charged artifact.

Positively engage the users by letting them create something personal related to their task. One car insurance website offered a tool that generated a cost range for a policy. Users could adjust basic settings to see what effect those choices had on the cost of insurance, such as the driver's age, ZIP code, and number of commuter miles. This initial estimate wasn't completely accurate, but it created a customized and tailored artifact.

This simple interaction allowed users to create a personally relevant artifact without forcing them to submit their email to request a quote. The design differed from the other insurance sites which required users to submit an email address to enable an agent to contact them with a detailed quote. Users were hesitant to request a quote from these sites—they knew they would receive lots of email spam or sales pitches after submitting their email address. Offering something personally relevant without a commitment (yet) gave the users confidence that they were going to get something worthy in exchange for their email.

The personal note card in the ProFlowers purchase flow is another good example of creating an emotional investment. When the customer selects a bouquet, rather than being immediately launched into the purchase sequence, they are asked to write a personal note to the recipient. By writing the note, customers become more emotionally tied to that purchase.

Once the note established the emotional engagement, it was quite successful in introducing an upsell, asking if the customer wanted to include a vase with the flowers. Usability testing showed that the interstitial upsell success was about five times higher with the note card and vase than the traditional method of asking the user to add the vase to a shopping cart.

Many websites offer whitepapers as a means to engage their visitors. Unfortunately, these whitepapers come at a cost: an email address. This "trade" represents a significant commitment by the users and is often a point of potential distrust. It's common practice to use that email address to not only share the whitepaper, but also to bombard the recipient with incessant marketing emails. These emails are often numerous enough to border on harassment. Many users abandon the whitepaper flow or provide fake contact information. Users are more likely to share something of value, like their email address, when they are certain that they are getting something of value *before* submitting.

It's a simple cost-benefit comparison. "What am I going to get in trade for the deluge of marketing emails I'm signing up for?" Additionally, companies are rarely honest about assurances that the users' email will be used properly. Users know this and *expect* to be spammed, so their cost-benefit calculations are based on this expectation. This is a high-commitment, low-perceived-value trade that scares many users off.

A more successful approach provides something personally relevant for a no- or low-commitment effort. The insurance quote example demonstrates this concept: it is perceived as a good trade because there is no real commitment by the user. It's just a few clicks without having to give up any personally valuable information. Once you deliver a personally relevant value proposition, asking the user if they want to save that result is fairly easy. At that point in the process, users would expect to be asked to create a username and password.

Create emotionally engaged interactions by delivering something intrinsically valuable without first requiring something even more valuable from the user.

Emotional Investment but No Payoff

Many years ago, Debbie Levitt worked on a project for a life insurance company that wanted their website to offer "three easy steps" to getting an insurance quote. Each step asked multiple personal questions about the user's life, health, and if they currently have life insurance.

At the end of the process, no quote was given, and the user was told that a representative would call them some time over the next few days. This was a huge disappointment and a broken promise since at the end of the "get a quote" flow, there was no quote. Many people did not prefer to talk to a salesperson.

The insurance company took up the users' time, and engaged them emotionally and personally, but failed to meet the users' payoff expectations. This type of disappointment creates a negative user experience for that company and all of its products. This is the kind of negative branding companies fear.

Emotional Investment Example: Custom Ink

The following set of screens from a previous version (2019) of the Custom Ink website (© CustomInk.com) demonstrates how to erode or create emotional investment. The task here is to create jerseys for a junior softball team. The members are kids of varying sizes and each child will have their own names and player numbers printed on their jerseys.

Notice how many screens the user must go through before reaching a point where they create something personally relevant that generates an emotional investment.

Figure 64: CustomInk.com landing page.

Is this page engaging? Does it instill a sense of emotional attachment?

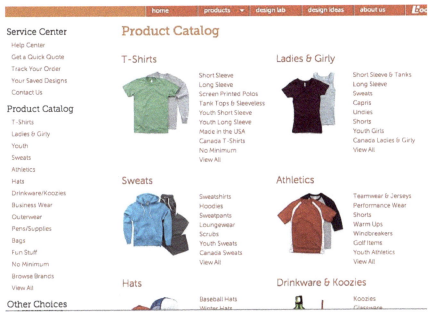

Figure 65: CustomInk.com product catalog page.

This is the first step after clicking, "Get Started." Is this emotionally engaging?

Figure 66: CustomInk.com T-shirt detail selections.

The next step in the process is still not emotionally engaging. The user has not yet made any investment.

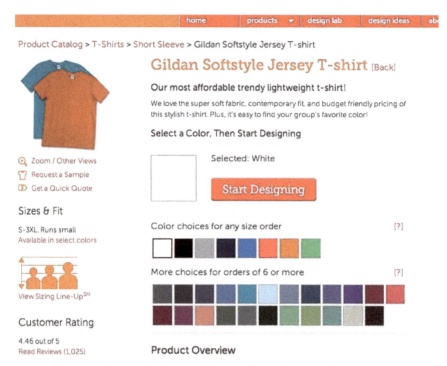

Figure 67: CustomInk.com short color selection.

Another non-engaging step of the process. This is getting a bit tedious.

Figure 68: CustomInk.com logo design page.

Finally! A screen where the user can create some emotional investment by creating something personally relevant, a logo.

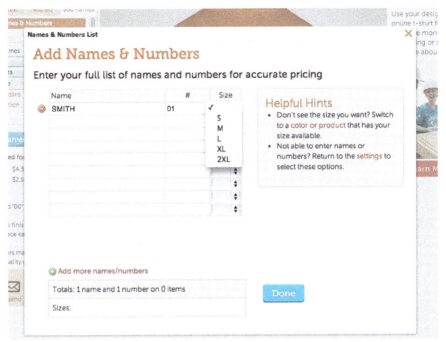

Figure 69: CustomInk.com player name and size entry with warning that some sizes may not be available in the shirt or color selected.

After creating or adding a logo design for their shirts, the user can then add names and player numbers for the team jerseys. This is another emotionally engagement opportunity.

But there's a hitch to this flow: the user is informed that not all of the shirts come in the sizes and colors they need during this size-selection step. This critical information is pointed out in the "Helpful Hints." It would have been more helpful to mention this issue up front, before the user went through this long process. The user now has to go back and repeat this process again and again until they find the right combination of colors, products, and sizes they need.

Here's an example of how to increase the potential for emotional investment and engagement, just by rearranging the order of the screens.

1. Start with the logo, design, or upload. That is the most relevant and emotionally charged artifact in this process.

2. Input the names and numbers that will go on the jersey along with that player's size. This is another emotionally charged aspect drawing the user into the process.

3. Pick the shirt colors for the team. This is another emotionally engaging step.

4. Since the system knows the sizes, quantities, and colors the user prefers or requires, the system can now show all of the shirt styles that have the right items in stock. The user is emotionally invested enough that they will continue the process, and it won't seem laborious.

We've also saved them from the potential problem of doing a lot of manual labor only to find that they can't have the shirts they wanted (which will feel like an error or wasted effort), and then being required to redo the work after selecting another shirt style.

Designing for Frequency of Use

The frequency of a user performing a task influences the design approach. If users are expected to perform their task more frequently, the design must be efficient to use. This efficiency comes at a cost, however: it relies on the users having more expertise or experience with this task, and may not protect against user errors as well.

If users are expected to perform the task infrequently, or if the task demands high accuracy, then consider focusing the design to prevent errors or promote ease-of-learning how to perform the task.

Designs that are focused more on high frequency tasks typically rely on greater user knowledge or experience with the product, and focus on reducing interactions to fewer steps to make the task more efficient. These kinds of designs are typically a little more difficult for the users to learn, but are optimized for reducing the number of interactions required to complete a task. Such a design typically lacks some of the design elements that help an uninformed or unfamiliar user for the sake of streamlining the task, and assumes that the user will have more knowledge given their repeated use. The result is a design focused on making the task steps quicker and more efficient to perform.

Designing for infrequent or unfamiliar tasks focuses on helping the user succeed with little to no training for an unfamiliar task. They won't have much experience or knowledge of this task, and rely on a design that guides them through the task. These types of designs typically include elements that initially help the user but become cumbersome if used repeatedly or frequently. They typically involve extra screens or many smaller steps, basically holding the user's hand during the task.

The U.S. tax software TurboTax is an example of a design that focuses on the infrequent user. The design uses a wizard-style interaction model that begins by asking users questions about their tax situation, such as how many children they have, how much income is reported, etc., and uses this information to identify which of the many tax forms the user needs to fill out. The design then walks users through the complicated form preparation process step by step, typically taking several hours or days. Given the complexities of filing income tax forms in the USA, this approach works well for users who are unfamiliar with the income tax filing process.

Consider how cumbersome this kind of wizard-interaction model would be for a professional tax preparer, who performs this task several times a day for months on end. They use a different software package that is much more streamlined to file their client's tax forms more efficiently. A professional might be able to complete a client's tax forms in an hour or two instead of days.

This doesn't mean that designing for ease-of-use and ease-of-learning is a binary, either/or choice, but suggests that sometimes the design must focus on one more than the other. It's possible for designers to achieve both easy-to-learn as well as easy-to-use objectives, especially with smaller products, such as a basic website or app. Achieving both ease-of-use and ease-of-learning is typically much more difficult for larger, more complex products. Attempting to achieve both in the same complex product usually incurs some expense of either or both objectives and is not recommended until you've had some practice.

Be Wary of the 3-Click Rule

For decades designers have rallied around the "3-click rule," which states that the desired results should be no more than three clicks away. For clarity, clicks here refers to any action a user takes to perform a task, be it turn a knob, flip a switch, click a button, etc.

The belief that a design or process should satisfy the user within three clicks is ineffective and just plain wrong. There are numerous cases where the design was fewer than three layers deep, but it still failed as a usable and useful solution.

Usability tests have proven that users don't need everything within three clicks as much as they need to know that *every* click brings them perceptibly closer to their desired outcome. Users commit an action with an expectation of what should happen. If the resulting response meets the users' expectations, and there is a perception of progress, the users will continue to click, even if an action takes five, seven, or even nine steps.

Focus the design on understanding the task flow the users expect to follow to achieve their objective. Relating the tasks to the user's mental model makes the perception of progress seem natural and expected, which keeps the user engaged and not thinking about how many steps they are taking.

Rather than fewer clicks, we should try to design for the right number of clicks. I've seen many cases where the designers focused on fewer clicks but made the users' task more difficult (too much to do on each page, increased user errors, higher cognitive demand, etc.). Task efficiency is more than just fewer clicks. It is a balance of more efficient task flows, managing user errors (and recovery), etc., without increasing the users' cognitive burden.

Start from the End

It is quite common for designers to start designing from the task's starting point and work towards the end. I've seen countless teams start by designing the login or account creation screens for apps or websites first. This approach automatically assumes that's where the users should start. However, that may not be the case. There are any number of tasks that users may want to complete that don't require a login. I've seen a number of websites that demand that users create an account before using a website. These designs perform very poorly. If you shouldn't start at the beginning, where should you start?

Sometimes it helps to start designing from the end of the task and work backwards, working from the desired outcome of the task flow backwards towards the initial trigger event. Rather than starting with the first page or screen of an app, design the end result first, then design the page that users interact with to generate that result, and so on, going backwards until reaching the trigger event that starts the task. Be sure to follow the optimized task flow to do this. You won't need to guess which screens you need since your optimized task flow is the map that will guide your design approach.

For example, in the custom T-shirt website, determine what the end state of the T-shirt order creation task should be (a list of T-shirts with the right colors, sizes, and graphics), and design that screen. Then determine which actions the users need to take to achieve that result, and design the screen that provides those actions (T-shirt type selection). Then design the screen before that (T-shirt color selection), and so on.

One thing to keep in mind when working backwards is to avoid including features that don't directly affect the next page or the desired outcome. Every element should be thoroughly considered before adding it to the screen. *Does it directly influence the right action for the user? Or is it just something cool that might have a possible use to some users?* This is the **what-if trap**: adding features in case a user *might* want to do something. Focus on the users' single task.

This approach is one way to ensure that your design achieves the desired outcome. More complex tasks with a lot of steps benefit more from this approach. You likely won't need to work backwards on simpler websites or apps where there might only be a couple of tasks and it's much more obvious what needs to be done.

Example Travel Project: Task-Oriented Design

Consider how a travel agent would approach organizing travel for a trip, which might suggest conducting some research with travel agents. They typically start with the departure and arrival locations in mind, and then work backwards from the desired endpoint while factoring in all of the intermediate travel options (subway, taxi, rental car, rideshare, etc.) to identify the realistic itinerary options. Then they present the traveler with the "best" option. If the traveler doesn't like that itinerary, they make adjustments until the traveler is satisfied.

Note that typical travel websites provide interfaces that are inconsistent with this common travel agent approach. Typical website travel design is a feature-oriented approach relying on the users to know how to look up various aspects of the trip in a disconnected fashion. Users typically use separate websites or interfaces for airplane travel, hotel accommodations, rental cars, etc.

Think of the system as the travel agent, and identify which steps can be accomplished by the system. The remaining steps would be performed by the user. The user starts by providing the beginning and ending points (not the airports, but the actual locations) as well as the desired arrival times for that final endpoint. The system then generates and delivers suggested itineraries including all aspects of the trip (plane, hotel, ground transportation, etc.) and provides screens for the user to adjust some specifics, such as no rental car, first class, etc. Each change results in a new itinerary.

This approach contrasts with the typical travel websites that separate each part of the travel event into unique steps, such as hotel selection, local travel options, and plane reservations, each as an individual step instead of a set of integrated steps of the travel task.

User Knowledge Profiles in Task-Oriented Design

Because user knowledge profiles are tied to specific tasks, when the user performs a task in a task-oriented design, we can accurately assume that this person embodies the user knowledge profile associated with that task. Remember that user knowledge profiles – unlike personas – are tied to specific tasks.

The design should avoid including controls and content that are unnecessary for that task and user knowledge profile. It should instead focus on providing just the controls and content that user knowledge profile requires to adequately perform the specified task.

For example, if the user interrupts their sales tracking task (sales manager profile) and selects a user admin task (admin profile) to add a new user to the system, then the system switches from the sales manager task-oriented design to the admin task-oriented design. Since sales tracking is a frequent task, the sales tracking UX design is optimized for efficiency (speed of use). The user admin task is an infrequent task, so the admin UX design must incorporate a more effective design approach (error avoidance, guidance) to help the user succeed. It's the same person, but different knowledge profiles, each performing a different kind of task that requires different design strategies (frequent vs. infrequent).

A feature-oriented design would list all of the features without regard for the frequency of the task and simply rely on the users to know how and when to use each feature. Focusing on the tasks rather than features creates designs that seem more intuitive to the different user knowledge profiles performing different kinds of tasks.

Chapter 15: Travel Example Design Approach

The following wireframes represent a notional approach to designing the travel-agent-oriented solution. It demonstrates how the system can create a single travel itinerary of connected travel modalities: rideshare to airport, flight, ride to hotel, hotel room.

Embedding knowledge into the design allows the system to provide Pat with various tips and directions as well as the various travel artifacts (boarding pass, subway directions, etc.) necessary to travel efficiently and effectively on a timely basis. For example, once Pat arrives in the New York City area, they are presented with wayfinding information to the subway, and to help them arrive where they need to be to complete the next step of their journey. Note that the application switches modality from using a laptop to make the reservations to a smartphone for navigating.

The following flow diagram illustrates how the associated wireframe screens map to the green sticky notes representing user actions in the previously described simplified example of the travel task flow, optimized diagram:

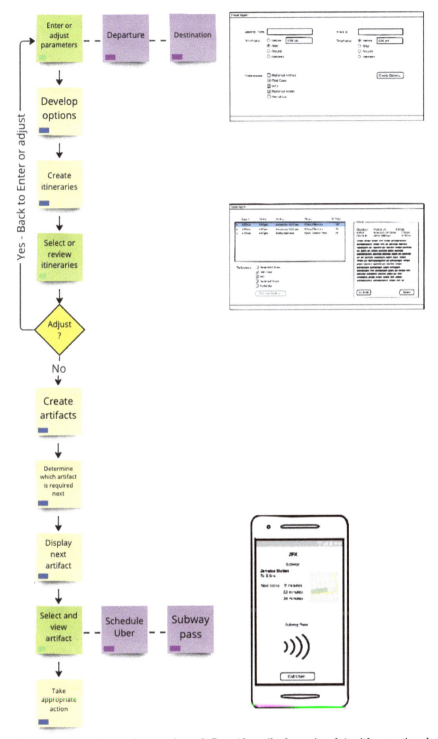

Figure 70: The optimized travel example task flow (described previously) with associated screen designs (described above) for the User (green) sticky notes in the task flow.

The simplified example of the travel task flow, Optimized:

- **User:** Enter or adjust parameters. **Artifact:** Departure, Destination.

- **System:** Develop options.

- **System:** Create itineraries.

- **User:** Select or review itineraries.

- **Decision:** Adjust? **Yes:** back to Enter or adjust parameters. **No:** go to next step.

- **System:** Create artifacts.

- **System:** Determine which artifact is required next.

- **System:** Display next artifact.

- **User:** Select and view artifact. **Artifact:** Schedule Uber, Subway pass.

- **System:** Take appropriate action.

Working backwards on the activity flow diagram below suggests designing the screen for the green sticky note at the bottom of the flow, first:

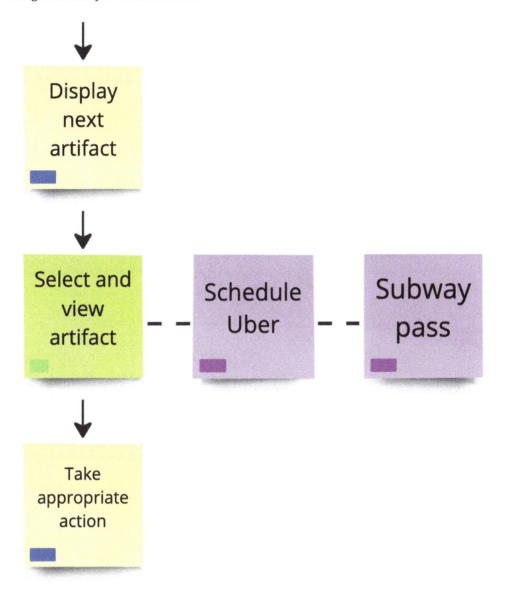

Figure 71: The final steps of the optimized travel example task flow to start designing backwards.

Final Steps Simple Travel Task Flow, Optimized:

- **System:** Display next artifact.

- **User:** Select and view artifact. **Artifact:** Schedule Uber, Subway pass.

- **System:** Take appropriate action.

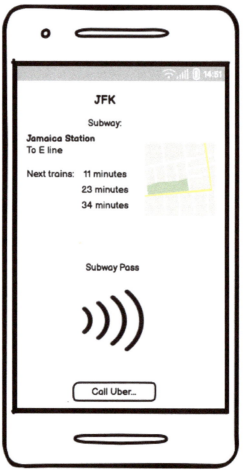

Figure 72: A rough smartphone wireframe for one of the last steps of the travel example task flow. It includes a map with directions to the subway, time before the next trains leave, and a way to pay for the subway ride from the phone. It also has a button to call for an Uber ride.

The smartphone is the modality used at the end of this journey. It's important to note that not all tasks will always be accomplished on a single platform. The artifacts displayed on the smartphone are the result of using the website on the user's laptop to arrange the travel, previously. Start with designing the screens for the last stage of the travel, that get the traveler to the hotel, such as providing the directions for getting from the airport to the subway station.

The following screen illustrates how the system will generate a few itinerary options that allow the user to adjust some parameters, if necessary.

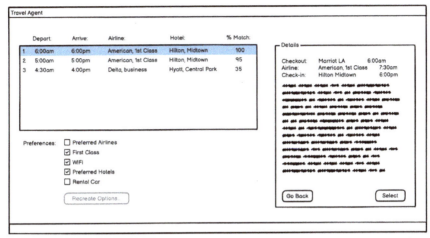

Figure 73: A wireframe of the itinerary selection screen of the travel example. It lists the possible itineraries (with a description of the selected itinerary), and allows the user to set travel preferences, such as First class, Wi-Fi, rental car, etc.

To generate these itineraries, the system will need to capture various travel parameters as illustrated on the following screen:

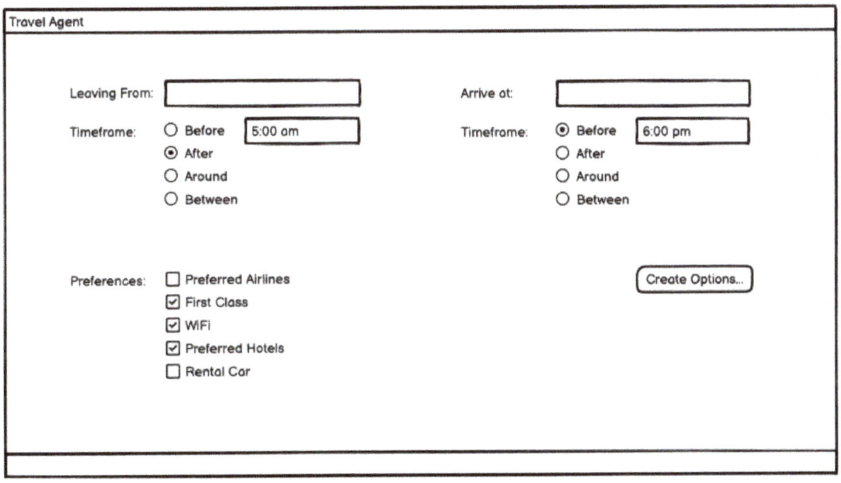

Figure 74: A wireframe of the starting point of the travel example task flow. This presents entry fields so the user can set departure and arrival times and locations, along with their travel preferences, as mentioned above.

Keep in mind that this is not intended to be a perfect solution at this early stage, but it should capture the design strategy enough to conduct some low fidelity usability testing.

Getting Buy-In for Task-Oriented Design

This step is intended to demonstrate the relationship of the designs to the task flows. Be ready to describe why this new design looks nothing like the previous design or the competitors' designs.

Share the wireframes or prototype screens next to the optimized task flow so people can see how they relate to the knowledge design.

By this point people will have a better understanding of the users and tasks and should provide some task-oriented feedback on the designs. That said, old ways can persist and there will be plenty of feature-oriented design suggestions. Remember, it may be tempting to add "cool" features, but you are not obligated to accept any of the suggestions. Evaluate every suggestion based on how well it fits the user and task.

Be prepared to discuss any objections people may have with the design. Rather than defending the design, listen their inputs and add them to the list of feedback. Remember, you are the one responsible for the success of the design, and it is up to you to determine what feedback applies to the design.

PART 7:   MORE DESIGN TIPS AND TRICKS

Rather than designing screens similar to your competitors, try identifying a design approach that drives the design towards a unique, more successful outcome. These tips are not directly related to the knowledge-design process per se, but leverage aspects of user psychology and behavioral science to help nudge users towards their desired outcomes. These approaches work for any type of product, service, or website, but for ease of discussion, this section focuses on website design.

The underlying principles of UX design are rooted in psychology and leverage what we know about human cognition to drive specific behaviors. Good UX design focuses on leveraging predictable user behaviors to compel site visitors to perform desired actions.

Chapter 16: The Four A's: Awareness to Action

Visitors come to a site with the intent to solve a problem. Contrary to popular website design approaches, users don't jump straight from a problem to purchase as soon as they visit a site. They typically do some research about their problem and the various solution options before buying anything. This is why expecting the user to click on the "Buy Now!" call-to-action button often doesn't work out so well.

Rarely do visitors come to a website intent on purchasing a specific product. Your site must convince visitors that your products serve their needs well enough to motivate them to purchase from it. The process is pretty straightforward but is rarely done well; visitors must transition through a mental process to determine whether the website offers the right solution, and if they want it.

This mental process is represented by the Four A's:

Figure 75: The four A's: awareness, attention, attraction, action.

1. **Awareness.** Visitors become aware of your product or service through your search-engine optimization (SEO), search-engine marketing (SEM), branding, and marketing efforts. These messages set expectations in visitors' minds about what they might find on your site.

   o One of the keys to establishing successful awareness is setting and managing appropriate expectations before they ever arrive at your site. Therefore, your marketing approaches must be in sync with your UX design efforts to ensure that users come to your site with appropriate expectations, and that you are able to meet those expectations.

   o When users land on your site, the first thing they look for is verification that they are on the correct site they intended to visit. Your outbound messaging sets an expectation about what the user will see on the website. If your messaging suggests that green widgets solve their kind of problem, users will expect to see green widgets when they land on your site. If the site does not reflect that messaging, and there are no green widgets, they might assume they are on the wrong site and leave.

2. **Attention.** Awareness drives visitors to your site, but it doesn't sell anything. Now that they've reached your site, you have only seconds to grab and hold their attention, the operative word being *hold*. The web is full of sites that can grab visitors' attention but fail miserably at holding it. Your site will hold the customer's attention if it expands on the awareness message, resonating with their problem.

   o In the 1990s, AT&T Cellular created eight billboard ads, each with a different message that included a URL for more information. Obviously, users weren't able to "click" on these URLs, but many users typed them into their computers later. They were presented with a homepage that showed the eight different billboard designs as thumbnails. This provided reassurance that the user had reached the right site. They could click on the billboard image they had seen earlier to open a page that provided more information specific to that message. Moreover, users would also click on other billboard images to see what else was there. This was a very effective campaign.

- ○ **What can we learn from that old example?** That there are various ways to set and meet user expectations, and that the message must be consistent with the website.

3. **Attraction.** Once you have their attention, the next step is to attract them to your product or service. Visitors often come to a site with some amount of uncertainty, and the goal of any site is to replace their uncertainty with a sense of desire. Once they desire your product, they are ready to take action, but they need one more thing before committing to your solution (described later).

4. **Action.** Once visitors decide to act, you just need to provide a frictionless flow through the task.

Transition Triggers

With that understanding of the Four A's, what does it take to transition the visitors through each of those stages? There are very specific triggers proven to nudge users through the Four A's. Unlike many marketing tools that leverage psychology in questionable and sometimes deceptive ways to elicit a behavior, these methods avoid crossing ethical lines and are intended to help the user solve their problem, rather than just leading them to buy something (that they may not really need).

Transition 1: Resonate with the User's Pain Point

Figure 76: The four A's indicating that a pain point transitions the user from awareness to attention.

Before your potential customers visit your site, they probably see your SEO, SEM, and branding and messaging efforts. These set expectations in visitors' minds about what they will encounter on the landing page. But these messages, keywords, and efforts should already be focused on users' problems and pain points, based on what we learned from our research.

Use what you know about visitors' pain points to establish and manage their expectations throughout their interaction with the site. Think about what drove them to your home or landing page. Visitors are more likely to visit and stay on the site when it's obvious that the company understands their needs and problems from their perspective.

At this early stage, avoid describing a solution. The outbound messaging should resonate with the user's problem. Rather than extolling the many features of the product, describe the common problems it solves. Users are more likely to listen when they hear someone talking about their problem.

For example, rather than listing all of the products and services the site offers (digital brochure), start by listing the top five to ten problems that people typically visit the site to solve. Users who recognize one of these problems as similar to theirs will investigate it, creating attention.

Transition 2: Demonstrate the Value Proposition

Figure 77: The four A's indicating that demonstrating the value proposition relative to the pain point transitions the user from attention to attraction.

Once you have your visitors' attention, you need to create enough desire and attraction to drive them toward an action. Your site must demonstrate the value proposition relative to their pain point. Visitors usually have some notion of what their desired outcome looks like, and your site must meet or exceed that ideal outcome. Sometimes you have a specific solution for their problem, and other times all you can do is indicate how you can help them identify a solution.

A common failure of many websites is to rely on visitor knowledge and skill to identify which features or solutions are right for them. Expecting the visitor to read all of the content, assimilate it, and reorganize it into meaningful knowledge places an undue cognitive strain on the visitor. In essence, you are expecting your visitor to become as knowledgeable about your products as you are, based solely on the provided content. This is impossible, futile, and utterly ineffective.

It is far more successful to organize the solutions as desired outcomes for the given pain points rather than as a generic list of solutions. Demonstrate that you understand your visitors' problems and have the right solutions for their needs by doing some of the work for them. Instead of asking them to read everything, ask them to identify some key issues they need to address, then provide just the right content or solutions specifically related to those issues. This may require the design to duplicate information to fit into multiple problems, but nothing says you can't or shouldn't duplicate information.

Kelly Blue Book (KBB.com) does this well with their self-identifying questions. The visitor identifies the question they want answered (buy or sell a car, private or dealer, etc.), and KBB.com presents just the right solution path. The result isn't a specific solution, but enough information to help the user solve their own problem.

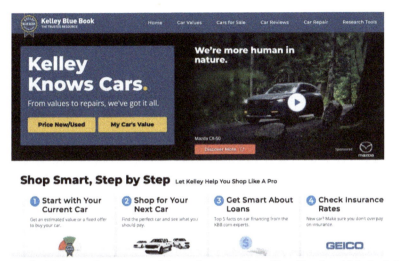

Figure 78: The KBB.com homepage with two buttons, Price New/Used and My Car's Value.

The actual Kelley Blue Book (named for the blue cover of their original book) is based around the vehicle (find the vehicle first, then add up all of the price adjustments based on features, mileage, condition, etc.), and presents several Blue Book prices for the described vehicle (buying a used car from a private party, buying from a dealer, trading in your car, etc.). The reader is left to determine the right price. The KBB.com website filters out the confusing, inappropriate prices and displays just the one that matches the user's calculated amount.

Transition 3: Give a Reason to Believe

Figure 79: The four A's showing that a reason to believe will transition the user from attraction to action.

By this time, the visitor is pretty much sold on your product or service, and merely needs to be reassured that you can accurately and easily solve their problem. They need a reason to believe. Common trust artifacts, such as testimonials, social proof (reviews), trust marks (association with known and trusted brands), awards, etc., all support their belief in your solution. They *want* to believe; you won't need to overwhelm them with these trust artifacts—just avoid scaring them away.

Finally: The Call-to-Action

Once the user has reached the action stage, they are looking for the appropriate call-to-action link or button. This is where the "Buy Now" button is most effective. The action must be contextually relevant for the current task, offering a single action that solves their problem. This approach is more successful than providing an array of options, commonly known as the paradox of choice, which creates additional cognitive effort and potential confusion.

The task-oriented design approach typically leads to a single appropriate action, therefore avoiding this paradox. If you find that you have several action choices to offer, then you may not have adhered to a task-oriented approach and are instead promoting a feature-oriented design. This should be your cue to reevaluate your problem definition and make sure you captured and followed a specific task flow. Ideally, the result should be one or two relevant solutions.

In This Exact Order

It's extremely important that you guide your visitors through these steps in this exact order. Too often, sites focus on the **reason to believe** by showcasing testimonials, awards, and client logos on the homepage before demonstrating an understanding of users' pain points or providing a valid value proposition. If the first thing visitors see on your page are reasons to believe, they might implicitly distrust your product, thus increasing the friction of transitioning them from awareness to attention or attraction. Don't tell them how great your company or product is until they know what it is and how it helps them.

Most visitors rarely convert on their first visit to a site. They usually go through a series of websites to compare and learn. A key objective is to make your site memorable. The Four A's approach creates a frictionless UX flow through the stages of awareness and produces positive emotions that improve visitors' recall memory, which makes it easier for them to want to return to your site.

ProFlowers Example

The outbound messaging for ProFlowers drives people to the website (awareness, pain point). Users typically visit the site because of a specific occasion. Although the homepage might be preselected for an occasion, such as a birthday, Valentine's Day, or Mother's Day, the users are presented with different occasions. This allows them to self-identify the problem they are trying to solve, which is *getting a gift for someone* (addressing the pain point).

Selecting an occasion presents a host of premade and appropriate bouquets. There is no guessing if the bouquet is the right kind, which demonstrates a knowledge-oriented solution or value proposition. The site includes several testimonials, trust marks, and reason-to-believe artifacts to drive the user to take action.

Note that the reason-to-believe was *not* the most visible thing on the site when the user landed on the page; the occasions were. The "Buy Now" button was provided on the screen that showcased the selected bouquet.

Create New Designs or Copy Familiar Ones?

A common question designers ask is whether or not the new design should look like the old design. The answer lies here:

- If it looks the same, it should behave the same.

- If it looks different, it should behave differently.

- If it behaves the same, it should look the same.

- If it behaves differently, it should look different.

Users take interaction cues from the interface design. If they see something similar to the previous design, their expectation is that the product will behave similarly, too. Imagine their surprise when the new design looks the same but behaves differently. It's very frustrating, and users will make more errors.

For example, I still see user interface designs that provide checkboxes that behave like radio buttons and vice versa. Users understand that a checkbox is inclusive (you can check multiple boxes), and radio buttons are mutually exclusive (you can select only one). They are confused when these common interaction rules are violated.

If the design behaves differently or follows a different mental model, the design must look very different as well, otherwise the users will transfer the old mental model to the new design. For example, if your new design's mental model is different, then your design must not look like the previous mental model. If the design is intended to behave the same, it should incorporate some familiar cues to set the right expectation in the user's mind.

Ideally, this task-oriented process will identify solution approaches that are completely different from anything that was done before. Therefore, if the design behaves the same or looks the same as before, then it very likely is the wrong design.

Chapter 17: Design for Common Search and Shopping Behaviors

Based on experience with various ecommerce and search-related products, users typically engage in a predictable manner when looking for something they know little about. A design that supports this predictable flow will perform better than the average online shopping or search model, where the users are expected to make a decision after making a single search.

Most websites commit the same mistake: failing to recognize and design for the fact that users typically do not make an important decision in a single visit. Important decisions are those key calls-to-action (CTA) such as purchasing, creating an account, starting a trial, or requesting a demo.

The most obvious indication of this failure is to have a CTA button on every page trying to drive the user to take that action. Users rarely buy a refrigerator on the first visit to a website, so why are sites so focused on getting them to "Buy Now" with a large, brightly colored button? Rather than asking the user to make a total commitment with a "Buy Now" button, the page could suggest additional actions that are more appropriate to helping the user through this process, such as "Calculate Your Needs."

With deep UX research, we can learn and understand the predictable process of the four or five steps a user might walk through before deciding to make a commitment. The more expensive or important a commitment is, the longer it takes for potential customers to shop or decide. It might take more steps or more time for the user to get the approval they need from a collaborator or someone who controls the budget.

A better approach recognizes that people typically go through several predictable cognitive stages before "pulling the trigger" on something. The more impactful the decision, the longer it takes and the more knowledge the user needs. Users tend to evolve their focus while gaining more knowledge about a product or service as follows:

Figure 80: Image illustrating the expand, saturate, narrow, and select flow.

Expand Their Knowledge

When a user begins searching for a solution, they likely won't know everything about the problem or solution space. This early stage of information gathering helps the users expand their knowledge of the domain and more accurately define their problem. Each new data point gives them more to think about and leads them into another direction of research. The more expensive or potentially harmful this decision is, the more they research it.

Saturate and Focus

Eventually the user reaches a point where they are not learning new information, and they begin to focus their attention on relevant issues regarding their problem. At some point, users stop learning and start determining the important factors and details about the options that the research uncovered. It's at this point that they start thinking about which products best fit into their priorities.

Narrow the Options and Prioritize

At some point the user feels like they have enough information to make an informed choice. They review the relevant choices and associated options to narrow down the list of acceptable solutions.

Their priorities help identify the two to three options that best serve their needs. Shoppers may review and modify their priorities several times while comparing the choices. One interesting thing to note is that sometimes they have a "gut response" to a specific choice and subtly bias the priorities to support that gut choice.

Service After the Sale

Not a specific single step, but a constant consideration that persists throughout this purchase process is what happens after the purchase is made. In ecommerce, this relates to the post-sale support or return policy.

Before many users commit to a specific solution, especially when the risk or cost is high, they like to know what experience they will have *after* the sale, such as return policy, product support, and maintenance and upgrade requirements of the product.

Many companies don't pay enough attention to this step of the process. Customers pick up various cues about the company or products to make sure that they will stand behind the sale and offer good customer service, even after the customer hands over their money. Including this information without expecting the users to ask for it is an example of providing knowledge that the user might not have or know enough to ask for.

Select

The user is ready to commit at this point, and makes a selection. This step might occur earlier, but they often still perform the successive steps, even if to justify their earlier decision.

How Does This Impact a Design?

A quick look at most ecommerce sites illustrates just how poorly they address these decision-making stages. The more stages that a site supports, the more likely the user will continue using that site.

Take a look at a site and objectively assess how well it supports these stages; the results will be surprising. One way to perform this quick analysis is to create a chart for each of the four stages, and place a sticky note representing each artifact or content supported in that stage. If there are stages that are not supported very well, there's an obvious problem.

How many websites provide the right features to serve those needs? Not many, if any at all. Some, like Amazon, offer some of the features, but not in a coordinated or intentional manner. Yes, they have reviews, but those are not organized to help the user flow through the shopping process. A well-planned website would perform even better.

Is Your Nametag Upside Down?

When speaking at conferences, I purposefully put my nametag on upside down. Invariably someone will point it out, "Larry, did you know your name tag is upside down?" I'll stop, look down at my chest and exclaim, "I can read it just fine from my perspective." Then people chuckle as I explain that most companies design their websites from their perspective, rather than their customer's viewpoint.

Companies design their website to reflect how they see themselves, not how their users see them. Users visit a website to solve a problem, but websites are typically organized around the solutions they offer, not the problems users have. They leave it to the user to read and assimilate all of the content to identify which parts of the solutions relate to their problem. More often this is because the designers don't know enough about their users to accurately describe their problems, and therefore don't know how to design a site that solves those problems.

We've all been to a site that we thought might help answer a question, only to be bombarded with a litany of blog posts, product descriptions, and sales pitches that fail to resonate with our pain point. Few people are willing to devote the time and energy to read through everything, determine which information relates to their problem, and then select from the many options for the best solution. Providing users with *all* of the information a company can scrape together about all of its products or services assumes that customers like to read and assimilate all this data in order to make a well-informed decision.

This information overload isn't how a company behaves in non-digital channels. Sales reps would never attempt to make a sale with one overwhelming email containing every product's details, specifications, or information. Then why should a website be designed that way? Think of a website as a type of sales rep. Mimic the non-digital sales process to increase the website's success. A website must be more focused on the users' needs rather than on the company's own products.

If a site is a catalog of solutions, typically organized by product models, then it's likely built based on how the company views its products. For example, a site might have pages for Widget A, which includes various models of Widget A. Then it could have another section for Widgets B, C, and so on. Obviously, there's a reason for having a Widget A-3, or a Widget A-7, etc. Each of those models solves a different problem. Instead of organizing the products by their model, organize them by the problems they solve.

When looking at a site or a design you're working on, does it offer solutions or does it solve problems? Is your name tag upside down?

Instructions Are a Symptom, Not a Solution

Instructions, training, help, and workarounds are symptoms of a design issue, not a solution. A design that requires instructions means it does not meet user expectations or fit the task very well. A good task-oriented design will not require any of these design Band-Aids.

The more instructions a design requires, the worse it is. It's a clear signal that this design isn't intuitive, and we're not sure the user will figure it out, so we need to lecture or train them. This also assumes that users will read (and understand) the instructions, which are often ignored.

Designers often create designs where it's obvious users won't know what to do, so they add instructions. Countless usability studies have proven that instructions don't work that well. Take the CustomInk.com example of instructions: they called them "Helpful Hints," but they were still instructions to help the user recover from a poor design.

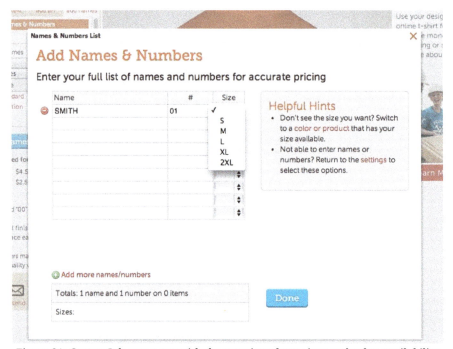

Figure 81: CustomInk.com page with the warning about sizes and color availability.

Adding instructions to a design is *not* the same as designing knowledge into the product. Instructions would not have helped users select the right bouquets on the ProFlowers site.

Too often, designers rely on these methods to compensate for some design shortcomings. Methods such as FAQs, Help, instructional videos, company training, and tooltips have shortcomings.

- **Tooltips** can be useful as long as the tooltip doesn't just repeat the object label. Examples of poor tooltips include a "Send" button with a tooltip that merely says "Send," and an email address field with a tooltip saying, "Enter your email address here." A better tooltip gives an example of what is required.

- **Overlays** that provide instructions for initial experience users can be effective, but should also follow a task-oriented approach rather than a functional reference description. A functional reference merely describes that the "Save" button does an action (saves the data). The information is just about the button, but not how that button fits into the task flow (it completes the entry, saves the data, and initiates the next step of the task). This is one method of supporting ease-of-learning for an otherwise ease-of-use design.

- **FAQs** are often misused. Some are constructed to convey marketing messages or the type of information you would get from a salesperson. FAQs assume that users want to hunt through a list of often disorganized questions to find one that matches their question. This is rarely a delightful experience.

- **Help** tends to provide functional reference help, indicating what a button does rather than how to complete a task. A better form of help would be more contextual, and describe how the object is used in completing the task at hand. This task-oriented help content design is much easier to design if the product follows a task-oriented approach as well.

- **Instructional videos and company training** should be focused on tasks as well. If the users need to be taught how to use the tool rather than how to perform the task, that is a clear indication that the product is not task-oriented.

Design with the intention of removing all of the instructions and instead use design cues that support the users' perception of the task and match their mental models. The best designs are logical, intuitive, "just work," and require minimal or no hints or training.

Now that you've created an initial design, it's time to test and refine it. Since the design is task-oriented, you can test just the parts of the design used to perform a specific task rather than having to wait for the entire design to be completed. This approach is especially useful for larger projects that might include numerous smaller tasks. The next section describes a novel method for conducting these task-oriented tests.

PART 8: TESTING THE TASKS

Chapter 18: Testing Task-Oriented Designs

One advantage of the task-oriented, task-analysis-driven design approach is that the observed tasks create the test tasks for usability testing a new design. This book began by stating that this knowledge-oriented UX methodology is a connected process, where every step is tightly coupled to and directly influences the next step. This approach to usability testing completes that connectedness by ensuring that the resulting design addresses the observed tasks that initiated this design effort, that you have solved the right problem well.

The typical test process is to conduct a test of the entire product rather than individual tasks. That's fine for smaller websites or apps, but more complex designs might benefit from a series of smaller tests, based on the tasks.

Testing the entire design all at once relies on the users using each part of the design correctly to complete their tasks. If they do something wrong in the first step, they likely cannot get through the next steps. This may not be as much of an issue for a small design like a small website, but can invalidate the testing of other parts of a larger, more complex enterprise product.

Rather than testing an entire design all at once, another option is to try testing specific parts of a design, one task at a time. The test tasks should be limited to specific interactions, flows, or mental models of a design. They should **not** be focused on individual features.

For example, instead of testing the entirety of a large ecommerce website, try testing the task of finding an interesting item. Then test how to continue shopping after adding items to the cart (you would be surprised how many cart designs make this task difficult), and finally test different aspects of the checkout sequences separately, such as using different payment methods. After testing and refining all of those tasks individually, then it makes sense to test the entire process for a final check.

If you have redesigned a minor part of the design based on the results of previous tests, it's not always necessary to waste time testing the rest of a design that seemed to work fine for the users. Running tests on just the tasks that required a redesign is a much more efficient use of your time. This is a more acceptable approach if the design change is rather minor, but a major design change might benefit from a full retest.

Designing a test based on the identified user tasks provides a much better idea of how well the design meets the users' mental models and how (or whether) we have solved their problems. For example, if the users had no trouble finding a birthday bouquet in a florist website, but struggled to find a "Happy Graduation" bouquet, then the design for where to find graduation bouquets might be an issue.

A feature-oriented design demands that the users know the process or action sequence to achieve an outcome: click button A, then D, then button C, then G, etc. A task-oriented design supports the right user actions down the right path (identified in the optimized task flow) by eliminating the unnecessary choices or features and providing the right choices or features at the right time.

Conducting a task-based usability test on a task-oriented design tests the task flow as well as the design, rather than just the users' ability to figure out which features to use. A task-based test avoids testing the user's knowledge, memory, or skills and instead focuses on testing your optimized flow and the design.

How to Write Test Tasks

One effective approach to usability testing involves disguising the actual objective of the test. For example, if the test objective is to determine how well the user can print something, rather than asking them to print a page, ask them something that results from printing a page, such as, "Does the app automatically add a page number on the printout?" This requires the test participant to print something, which is the actual test objective, but they won't know that.

Disguising the true objective of the test reduces the likelihood of the user changing their behavior to "game" the test. It is well known that users want to appease the tester, so they will try harder than they normally would in real-world task environments. This approach of disguising the true objective avoids that user bias.

As another example, some researchers believe that the best way to test a system's user onboarding experience is to ask people to go through the experience. These researchers want to then ask questions about the onboarding like, "Did you like it?" (which doesn't mean it's good) or, "What do you remember about the onboarding process?" (which doesn't mean they will remember anything the next time they use your system).

The best way to test an onboarding experience is to give people a task that happens after the onboarding, and watch what they do. Do they skip the tutorials? Do they make mistakes? Does the onboarding warm them up for their task or seem to stall or block it? Use your observational skills to determine what onboarding is truly like, especially when the participant doesn't know that's what you're watching for.

For example, if an initial task that occurs after onboarding is to create a folder in the system, instead of asking the users to "create an account and login to the system," ask them if the system allows them to create a junk folder once they login. They will think that the junk folder is the objective of the test, but in fact it's the onboarding flow.

Notice that the test task was phrased as a question ("Was there a page number on the printout?") rather than a statement. Rather than giving a command, try getting users to perform a task by asking questions. Asking a question instead of giving an order or command produces a more intrinsic motivation than a laborious task statement ("print several pages and look for a page number"), which sounds like work.

It is not uncommon for a user to try a little harder than normal if given a command to complete a task, thus creating inaccurate observable data. If they are presented with a question, they often feel it is okay if the answer is "no," and will not try harder than they normally would if performing this task at home or work. Their behaviors tend to be more natural and authentic, and produce more reliable results.

This simple technique also avoids implying that the test task is doable. If the user struggles with the task, the moderator can simply state that this part of the design or prototype has problems or limitations. "Thank you for showing us the problem, we can go on to the next question now." I've seen participants try over and over when told to do something because they didn't want to fail, which they admitted in the post-test interviews.

Avoid making subsequent tasks dependent on a previous result. If the user doesn't complete the first task, they won't be able to accurately perform a second task that relies on the result of the first. Change the test slightly so that they start a subsequent task with all of the correct artifacts (information specific to the tasks, such as addresses, phone numbers, etc.) they need.

The advantages of this approach increase with larger, more complex websites, products, or services. This method breaks tasks down into smaller components so that users are not overwhelmed with an otherwise long, difficult task. Breaking the test down into smaller tasks also avoids the issue of user errors early in the test sequence adversely affecting later tasks.

This test task approach ensures all of the users will see and use the same parts of the design. An open-ended test, such as telling the user to buy something on an ecommerce site, does not ensure that all of the users will visit the same pages and use the same features. Having the users follow the same task sequences ensures that you get more data on the parts of the design that you are interested in. Of course, it can be rightfully argued that it is still important to note how and why users went in unexpected directions.

There is some concern that this may be leading or priming the users, but in complex systems, the opportunity for the users to go off-track and click outside of the intended task area means that you will have to test with far more users if they are not constrained to some extent. If you test with ten users and seven of them get lost going into areas that aren't part of the test objective, then you end up with only three data points regarding your task of interest. This is not enough to accurately draw a conclusion, and you would need to test with more users.

Of course, if seven out of ten test participants go off-track, that is an indication that something about the design led them off-track, and deserves investigation.

The opposite problem is to constrain the users or lead them so much that it essentially invalidates the test. You want to avoid giving them hints in the test task, such as using terms that are in the design. "Does clicking the 'Save' button actually save your thing?" suggests that the user should click the "Save" button. This could be rewritten as, "Is there a way to make the system update with your changes?"

One way to address the off-track type of problem is to use a prototype that indicates that the part of the design where a user might go off-track is not designed yet. You can suggest that they try another way to complete the task. I've used pop-ups that say "This part isn't done yet. What do you expect it to do?"

Test Scenario Planning

If you are testing a design that relies on users succeeding on the first attempts, such as an ecommerce site, then the test tasks are typically pretty straightforward, and should focus on the participants' initial reactions to the design.

While it's always a goal to make the design both easy to learn and easy to use, it's not always possible with larger, more complex applications. You will likely need to prioritize which design objective to focus on, efficient or effective. Writing a test scenario for a design that focuses on ease-of-use (making the user more efficient) could follow a format to test each task several times. This provides multiple data points to indicate how well or quickly the users learn and understand the design approach.

For example, when testing a design that relies on the users to use, edit, or create an unfamiliar artifact, you can create three versions of the test task. The first version could be to introduce some artifact by asking the user to identify some characteristic of it (use). The second version of the same task could get the user to modify a similar artifact (edit). The third version of that task could be to create a similar artifact from scratch to demonstrate actual knowledge (create). This should provide enough data points to determine the learning curve of the design, how easily the user can understand it correctly. If the users all seem to struggle with the same version of the test, this provides a fairly good idea of where to look for a problem.

Using variants of the same task helps avoid the bias of task familiarity. Repeating the same exact task tests the user's ability to remember how that task was performed. If the task includes sufficient variation, the user will be required to think it through. How much is sufficient is dependent on the users and the tasks. This is something you should look for in the pilot tests.

This multi-step approach isn't always necessary for simple things like a small website, but it works well in identifying design issues for more complex products. I once tested a design for medical billing coding tasks. The users were all experienced billing coders who performed this task 8 hours a day. I created test scenarios which repeated coding tasks several times to determine how well the design fit their mental model.

Interestingly, the coders took a couple of attempts before they realized this was a different design approach from their previous software and acclimated to the new design. Their comments suggested that the new design better fit their mental model, but they didn't realize it at first due to their familiarity with and expectations of the old software.

Each test task should be slightly more complicated than the previous one. The following describes a common test plan:

- **First** introduce the task with a simple test, such as reviewing something. For example, ask them if the website has a specific value in a form.

- **Second,** use a more complex test such as editing something. For example, ask them what they can do if that field has the wrong value in it.

- **Third,** use an even more complex task, such as creating something. Tell them they need a new form similar to the form they just edited.

This provides three data points of a single task type to draw a curve showing comparable user performance for the same task. Remember, the goal is not to test individual features, but the set of features that supports a given task or mental model.

Moderating the Tests

Rather than speaking with the participant and giving them tasks or questions, I prepare a binder with all of the questions written down for the participants and have them work through the binder. I ask them to write their answers down on the pages. This gives me a clear indication that they believe they have completed that part of the task. It is acceptable to converse with participants who have difficulty reading the questions or writing their answers.

When testing remotely, you may be able to provide the "binder" as a document that they can enter their answers. Also, some users may have difficulties with written instructions (vision, dyslexia, or language issues) in which case, you may need to present the questions verbally. These are just some of the issues that can arise, just be respectful of people's needs and accommodate as well as you can.

This approach limits the degree of interaction I need to have with them (and therefore avoids influencing the participants), which can interrupt their thought processes. Of course, I remind them to think aloud now and again. Keep in mind that going quiet and forgetting to think aloud may be an indication of a cognitive friction point. It can also be that they've gotten into the cognitive flow and are doing well and want to keep going. I try to avoid interrupting them when they are doing well and limit interruptions to helping them through a friction point, if necessary.

If the participant is struggling, I won't give them the "answer" but might ask questions that might suggest a specific insight about the interface. Sometimes I simply remind them that this is just a prototype and it has some glitches. I can then move them on to the next task.

Example Test Task

To test the navigation and content on a travel destination tour website, rather than tell the user to just look at the content for a specified destination, ask them which of three suggested destinations would be more interesting to them. This will intrinsically motivate them to search for things using more natural behaviors to seek something more personally relevant to them.

Once they indicate which one is more interesting, ask them something specific about that destination that can only be answered by using the travel site. Then ask them which other destination offers something similar. This keeps them intrinsically motivated to complete the task, rather than merely following orders, and provides a more natural behavior data point. This approach gives you an idea of how well the users naturally use and understand the design approach.

A key difference between this task-based approach and the traditional approach is that the organic user behaviors observed in the traditional test provide data about how easy it is to learn a design, but not necessarily how easy it is to use efficiently. You can identify the ease-of-use aspects by repeating similar tasks and comparing each user's relative behavior metrics, such as error rate or time on task, across those tasks.

You can't accurately compare one user to the other, but you can compare the performance of the same user across the various tasks. If the user makes the same error in all three versions of the same task, that's an indicator that there is an issue in that part of the design. If you see the user performance improve dramatically in the three test tasks, you can feel confident that the design is good. This can be explored in the post-test interviews.

Protect the Participant

It's important to introduce the test tasks by telling the participants that there are known issues with the design or the prototype. This can be useful to get them past a troublesome part of the design. When the participant struggles with a part of the design, thanking them for finding one of the known issues with the prototype helps prevent them from feeling like they failed. Moreover, they feel like they are helping test the product, which is true, rather than the test being focused on them.

As mentioned earlier, this illustrates the importance of using questions to guide the testing rather than commands. Telling the participant to "print something" implicitly suggests that the printing function works, and if they can't print, it's their fault. Asking a question leaves the possibility open that the system is at fault, not the user.

Some Evaluative Testing Limitations

The following two common approaches are viable evaluative research testing methods, but they don't support a knowledge-oriented generative research approach. They both require a design and if that design has not benefited from this approach, it is likely solving the wrong problem. The best you hope to achieve is solving the wrong problem very well.

Testing an Existing Design

Usability testing an existing, live-to-the-public design, such as a competitor design or your own current design, typically identifies that it doesn't solve users' problems well. Therefore, it is not the correct design, but the research already suggested that. Usability testing rarely leads to innovation; it's more likely to lead to incremental, evolutionary changes to the design. While you must sometimes fix or improve a design, usability testing is unlikely to point you in an innovative, generative direction.

Testing an existing design as a generative process assumes that it solves the right problem to begin with, which is typically an inaccurate assumption. Testing an existing design constrains the observations to the context of the current design.

Usability testing provides an evaluative analysis of a design to determine how well (or poorly) it supports the user's tasks. This is not generative research that identifies unique, revolutionary, or innovative insights. You need to conduct generative qualitative research to learn enough about users and their tasks to create something revolutionary.

A/B Testing

The A/B testing method is a way to measure the ability of a single change to create a notable impact. This is why it's often used in optimization; change one thing, see how that impacts the user's performance, make another small change, and so on.

Eventually, A/B testing will reveal the best design for doing one thing, but it doesn't identify if that is the right thing to do. It won't reveal that B attempts to solve the wrong problem, especially if we find that B created a KPI lift that we were hoping for. Option B might be the best design for achieving business goals, but it could create a poor user experience or work against users' goals.

Imagine you are climbing a mountain in dense fog. You keep going up until you can't find a trail that goes up anywhere. You exclaim that you have finally reached the summit. When the fog lifts, you find that you are only at the top of a hill next to the mountain. You actually need to go down the hill to reach the mountain and start climbing again.

A/B testing typically results in just such a local maxima, a point within a certain range that is higher than other points nearby, giving false confidence that you have achieved the highest point.

Not all A/B testing is flawed, but it is often performed inaccurately, or at the wrong time with the wrong purpose. You can't A/B test your way to innovation, and you're unlikely to A/B test your way to increased customer satisfaction. The most troubling use of A/B testing is when the "hypothesis" is really a guess, something someone hopes will get users to do what the business wants.

Additionally, A/B testing often leads to an entirely incorrect product strategy or no strategy. The example of my research leading to ProFlowers' overarching UX strategy becoming "ProFlowers doesn't sell flowers; they sell occasions" reminds us that great research doesn't just deliver findings, insights, and opportunities: it delivers business intelligence that can be used to create or influence actionable company and product strategies, goals, and initiatives.

Chapter 19: Test Tasks for Our Sample Travel Project

The key to good testing is to avoid testing the entire product or task flow in one single test right away, and instead break the test into smaller tasks. You can test the entire task later once you have user performance data on the various sections. Also, since this example travel scenario is a task many business travelers will perform multiple times, this is designed more for efficiency rather than effectiveness and will likely require a series of test tasks of increasing complexity (use, edit, create).

After providing the test scenario ("You are Pat..."), ask the user questions that can only be answered by using the prototype. Be sure to provide all of the data and artifacts (neighborhoods, hotel addresses, etc.) they will need to perform the tasks.

Tasks for your test(s) would include:

- Identify your starting or origin location.

- Identify your final destination and desired time to arrive.

- Indicate specific travel parameters such as a first-class flight, Wi-Fi on the plane, rental car not required, etc.

- Review itinerary options the system provides.

Remember to use questions to guide the user rather than direct statements. This develops a more natural and intrinsic motivation to perform the task, and the user is less likely to feel like a failure if the "system" doesn't work right.

A test plan might look like this:

- **Test Scenario:** You are Pat, an executive currently in Los Angeles (LA) for a client event. You just learned that you need to be in New York City (NYC) the next evening... [the rest of the scenario here].

- **Test Task 1:** What does the system use as the default the starting point for this trip? The address of your last known location (such as the hotel you are currently staying at), your current location (such as the coffee shop you are currently in), or does it require you to enter a location?

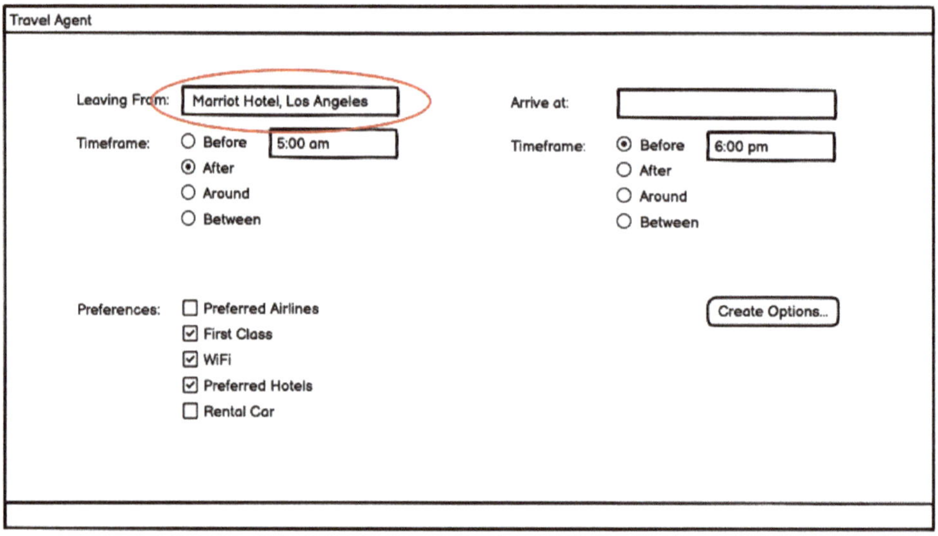

Figure 82: The travel example screen to enter current location and destination with Current location highlighted to show "Marriott® Hotel, Los Angeles" prefilled in the entry field. The red oval is for illustrative purposes, to show which field this task is referring to. Don't include such a highlight on the prototype screen.

- **Test Task 2:** Does the system accept general locations for the final destination, such as a hotel name, or does it require a specific address?

- **Test Task 3:** Do you need to indicate specific options such as first class, Wi-Fi, etc., before, after, or both when searching for available itinerary choices?

- **Test Task 4:** Does the system add a whole new itinerary if you change your final destination to a hotel brand in midtown Manhattan, NYC, or just update an existing itinerary?

- **Test Task 5:** If you suggest a 10:00 a.m. start time, does the system alert you that it will not get you to NYC in time for dinner?

These are examples of test task questions that prompt the users to perform various tasks. Note that tests 1 and 4, and 2 and 5 test the same task twice, only slightly differently.

This concludes the knowledge-oriented design process. You likely have unanswered questions, but don't be afraid to give this process a try. After some practice, try experimenting with some of the methods to fit them to your website, product, or service. No two of my projects were performed the same way, and I am continually learning more things to try with each project.

Getting Buy-in for Usability Testing

Sometimes it helps to highlight a few key usability test findings, especially if there were competing designs or if someone suggested a design approach that was tested. This helps reinforce the trust that the design team is listening and that it values everyone's input.

Share the wireframe designs with indications of which problems were uncovered and addressed. Try sharing a schedule of tests, inviting others to observe a few of these. This should include a description of the test process and what to expect, to avoid observers confusing usability testing with the more common user testing, which is a functional test of the technology.

After a while, people will stop talking about features and talk about tasks. You'll know you've really done well when people in your company want to watch some of the usability tests.

A note of caution: it's not uncommon for people to see just one test and think they can solve all of the observed difficulties. Remind them that they need to observe multiple tests and avoid generalizing on a sample set of one.

PART 9: IN CLOSING

Chapter 20: The End

There are countless books describing variations on a theme of common user experience design methods, many of which focus on creating artifacts like personas and empathy maps. Some promote *speed over quality* UX processes, such as *Lean UX*, but none describe all of the methods presented in this book.

Other methods rarely generate the repeatable kinds of successes knowledge-oriented UX methods have achieved. If these common methods really worked, there would be many more successes rather than the ubiquity of mediocre designs. Methods that are currently trendy claim they "work" by saying that people enjoy doing these methods or create "design thinkers." We should judge our processes and methods by outcomes: tangible metrics such as conversion rates, lead generations, customer retention rates, etc., and not by how much fun we had or how "collaborative" we all felt while coming up with the wrong solution.

Most designs measure successes by small increments, such as a 0.25% lift in conversions or gaining 2% market share, but this knowledge-oriented UX process has led to successful designs that achieved truly market dominating successes far beyond the minor incremental results of typical UX methods.

The stellar successes of this process include some of the highest website conversion rates (10%-25%), setting the standards for entire industries, creating entirely new industries, and generally exceeding everyone's expectations. It's hard to find another UX approach with as many extraordinary success stories covering so many different domains: extremely profitable websites, highly productive enterprise software, gold-standard medical device designs, and more.

As of the writing of this book, Artificial Intelligence is not yet sophisticated enough to achieve these kinds of results. As you might guess, current AI capabilities cannot perform the types of activities or gain the insights that achieve the successes described here. For that matter, the current attempts of using AI to create synthesized representations of users and their needs are inaccurate enough to warrant caution in using AI, for now.

Even though it is highly successful, this knowledge-oriented process is not perfect. Born out of Don Norman's User-Centered Design classes and evolved over several decades and hundreds of projects, these knowledge-oriented research and design methods are guidelines and a basis for experimentation. Every project is different, and no single process can solve every problem perfectly. Don't be afraid to try doing things a little differently, and see what kind of results you can generate.

Chapter 21: Resources

- **DeltaCX.Media**. This is the second book in our new publishing imprint, Delta CX Media. More to come! Check out our other titles.

  o This site includes books, authors, video courses, and live workshops.

  o We also have items for sale directly from authors such as signed books.

- **Download the PDF of Images**. Many of you will want access to the images in this book in a format where you can zoom in and see more detail. Please visit https://deltacx.link/dr-images for all of the images and examples herein.

Chapter 22: Thanks and Acknowledgments

Thanks to so many people for their work on this book. Some spent hours, if not days or weeks, helping with the editing.

Thanks to Super Editors

These absolute champions were content editors, structural editors, line editors, copy editors, and proofreaders.

- **Debbie Levitt** [https://linkedin.com/in/debbielevitt/], who also ghostwrote some of the book.

- **Linda Hwang** [https://linkedin.com/in/lindahhwang/]

Thanks to Content Editors

- Cherish Clark [https://www.linkedin.com/in/cherishclark/]

- Karen Davtyan [https://www.linkedin.com/in/karendavtyan01/]

- Matteo Gratton [https://www.linkedin.com/in/matteogratton/]

- Kelene Lee [https://www.linkedin.com/in/kelenelee/]

- Uddipta Mahanta [https://www.linkedin.com/in/uddipta-mahanta/]

- Maia Naftali [https://www.linkedin.com/in/mnaftali/]

- Michelle Pakron [https://linkedin.com/in/michellepakron/]

- Irena Pavlovic [https://www.linkedin.com/in/irena-pavlovic/]

- Shaleen Sachdeva [https://www.linkedin.com/in/shaleensachdeva/]

Thanks to Chris Lenhart

The *attractive* graphics in this book were designed by Chris Lenhart [https://www.linkedin.com/in/chrislenhart72/]. The rest are screenshots from Larry's archives and Miro boards.

Chapter 23: Index

Chapter 24: Appendix: Full Travel Example

The entire travel example project is provided here to illustrate the continuity of the research and design artifacts.

Travel Example Scenario

Pat is an executive currently in Los Angeles (LA) for a client event. They just learned that they need to be in New York City (NYC) the next evening for a client dinner. Pat has never been to New York City, and is unsure of where things are and how to get around. The client dinner will be at 7:00 p.m. in midtown Manhattan, and Pat will want to stay in a nearby hotel.

Because of evening commitments in Los Angeles, Pat can't take a red-eye flight (common U.S. slang for an overnight flight). How does Pat figure out their NYC travel plans?

Issues Pat needs to address include:

- How early to leave the hotel in Los Angeles.

- How to get from the hotel to the Los Angeles (LAX) airport.

- Which airport to use in NYC. There are three: EWR (Newark), JFK (Kennedy), and LGA (LaGuardia).

- Which flights have first-class seating available.

- Which flights have Wi-Fi so Pat can research the new client and feel prepared for the dinner meeting.

- The best NYC hotel for Pat's needs. Pat focuses on their preferred hotel brands and airlines to reduce the search effort.

- How to get from the NYC airport to the hotel. Should Pat rent a car in NYC?

Note that this list does not specify which websites were used or how they were used. We have only detailed what Pat is trying to accomplish. We are solution-agnostic, and would observe many people matching Pat's profile as they use various sites and solutions.

Travel Task Flow, First Pass

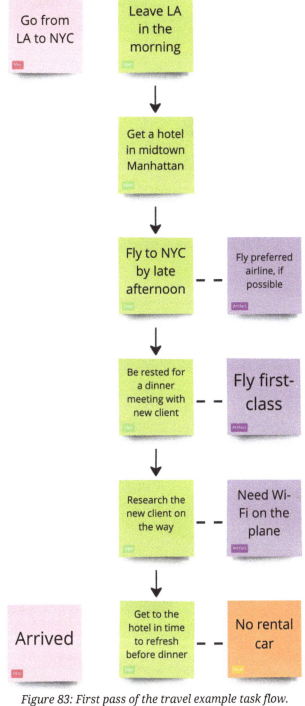

Figure 83: First pass of the travel example task flow.

Travel Task Flow, First Pass:

- **Misc**: Go from LA to NYC. **User**: Leave LA in the morning.

- **User**: Get a hotel in midtown Manhattan.

- **User**: Fly to NYC by late afternoon. **Artifact**: Fly preferred airline, if possible.

- **User**: Be rested for a dinner meeting with new client. **Artifact**: Fly first class.

- **User**: Research the new client on the way. **Artifact**: Need Wi-Fi on the plane.

- **Misc**: Arrived. **User**: Get to the hotel in time to refresh before dinner. **Issue**: No rental car.

Travel: Task Flow Second Pass

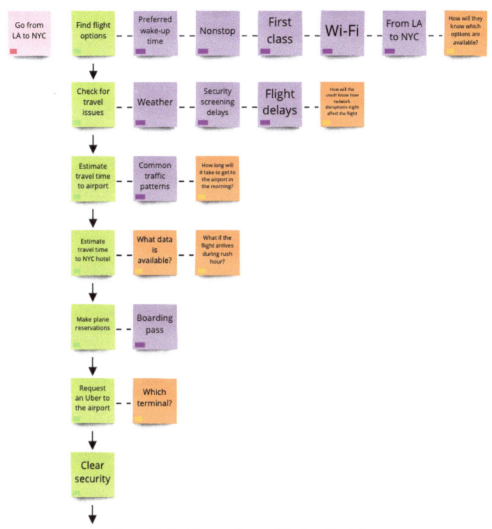

Figure 84: Part 1, second pass of the travel task flow.

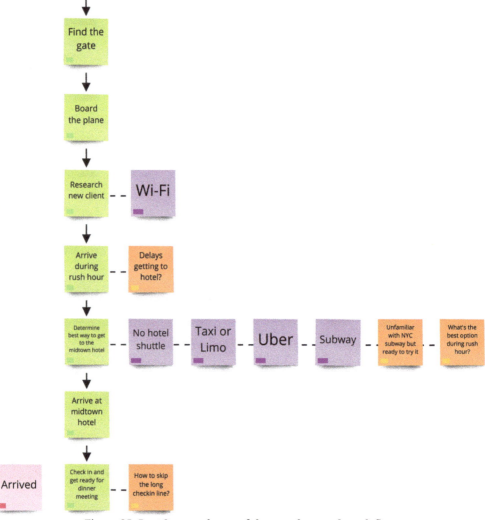

Figure 85: Part 2, second pass of the travel example task flow.

Travel Task Flow, Second Pass:

- **Misc**: Go from LA to NYC. **User**: Find flight options. **Artifact**: Preferred wake-up time, Nonstop, First class, Wi-Fi, From LA to NYC. **Issue**: How will they know which options are available?

- **User**: Check for travel issues. **Artifact**: Weather, Security screening delays, Flight delays. **Issue**: How will the user know how network disruptions might affect the flight?

- **User**: Estimate travel time to airport. **Artifact**: Common traffic patterns. **Issue**: How long will it take to get to the airport in the morning?

- **User**: Estimate travel time to NYC hotel. **Issue**: What data is available? What if the flight arrives during rush hour?

- **User**: Make plane reservations. **Artifact**: Boarding pass (within 24 hours of departure).

- **User**: Request an Uber to the airport. **Issue**: Which terminal?

- **User**: Clear security.

- **User**: Find the gate.

- **User**: Board the plane.

- **User**: Research new client. **Artifact**: Wi-Fi.

- **User**: Arrive during rush hour. **Issue**: Delays getting to hotel?

- **User**: Determine best way to get to the midtown hotel. **Artifact**: No hotel shuttle, Taxi or limo, Uber, Subway. **Issue**: Unfamiliar with NYC subway, but ready to try it, What's the best option during rush hour?

- **User**: Arrive at midtown hotel.

- **Misc**: Arrived. **User**: Check in to hotel and get ready for dinner meeting. **Issue**: How to skip the long check-in line?

Traveler User Knowledge Profile

- **Trigger.** Unexpected client dinner in New York City.

- **Desired outcome.** Must be there, refreshed, and ready to meet a new client for dinner in midtown.

- **Common knowledge.** Knows how to use different travel methods and sites. Knows to not rent a car in NYC.

- **Required knowledge.** Which NYC airport to fly into, which hotels are in midtown, how to get from NYC airport to midtown.

- **Knowledge gap.** Has never been to NYC and doesn't know how to get from the airport to their hotel in midtown Manhattan.

Name: Traveler Pat

Objective:
Make it to dinner with the
new client in NYC

State of Mind:
A bit anxious

Trigger:	Gets notified late in the day before another client dinner
Outcome:	Be on time for dinner, refreshed and prepared to meet the new client
Common K_n:	Knows how to travel and use subways or Uber to get around. Knows not to rent a car in NYC.
Required K_n:	Which NYC airport to fly into, which hotels are in midtown how to get from NYC airport to midtown
K_n Gap:	Never been to NYC and doesn't know their airports or subway systems
Artifacts:	Airports, busses, subways, passes, airport check-in, hotel check-in

Figure 86: The user knowledge profile for Pat.

Travel Task Flow, Optimized

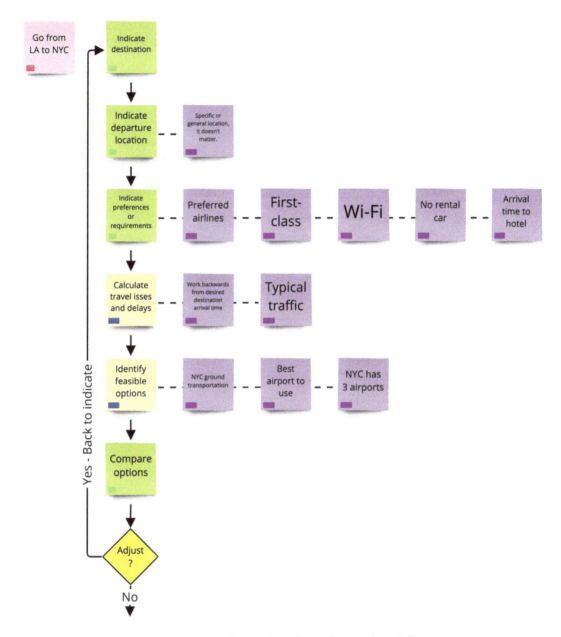

Figure 87: Part 1, detailed optimized travel example task flow.

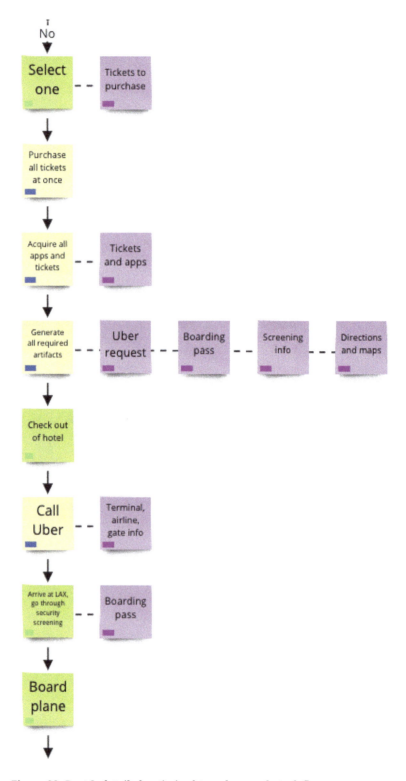

Figure 88: Part 2, detailed optimized travel example task flow.

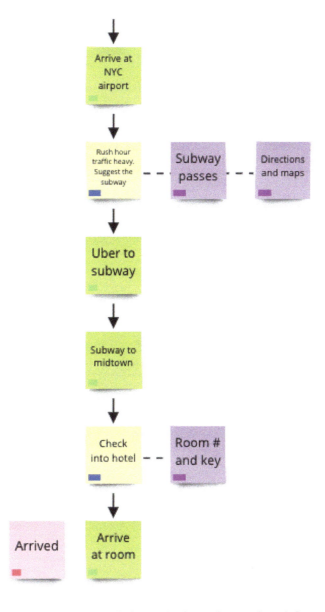

Figure 89: Part 3, detailed optimized travel example task flow.

Figure 90: Legend of the sticky note colors: User (green), System (yellow), Issue (orange), Artifact (purple), Misc (pink).

Travel Task Flow, Optimized:

- **Misc**: Go from LA to NYC. **User**: Indicate destination.

- **User**: Indicate departure location. **Artifact**: Specific or general location, it doesn't matter.

- **User**: Indicate preferences or requirements. **Artifact**: Preferred airlines, First class, Wi-Fi, No rental car, Arrival time to hotel.

- **System**: Calculate travel issues and delays. **Artifact**: Work backwards from desired destination arrival time, Typical traffic.

- **System**: Identify feasible options. **Artifact**: NYC ground transportation, Best airport to use, NYC has 3 airports.

- **User**: Compare options.

- **Decision**: Adjust? **Yes**: back to Indicate destination. **No**: go to next step.

- **User**: Select one. **Artifact**: Tickets to purchase.

- **System**: Purchase all tickets at once.

- **System**: Acquire all apps and tickets. **Artifact**: Tickets and apps.

- **System**: Generate all required artifacts. **Artifact**: Uber request, Boarding pass, Screening info, Directions and maps.

- **User**: Check out of hotel.

- **System**: Call Uber. **Artifact**: Terminal, airline, gate info.

- **User**: Arrive at LAX, go through security screening. **Artifact**: Boarding pass.

- **User**: Board plane.

- **User**: Arrive at NYC airport.

- **System**: Rush hour traffic heavy, suggest the subway. **Artifact**: Subway passes, Directions and maps.

- **User**: Uber to subway.

- **User**: Subway to midtown.

- **System**: Check into hotel. **Artifact**: Room # and key.

- **Misc**: Arrived. **User**: Arrive at room.

Travel Project Matrix

Function/Task	User Experience	Business	Tech Feasibility	Overall
Indicate destination	2			
Indicate departure location	2			
Indicate preferences/requirements	1			
Calculate traffic issues/delays	3			
Compare flights	2			
Compare hotels	3			
Compare itineraries/options	3			
Adjust itinerary details/preferences	2			
Select/purchase an itinerary	1			
Create itinerary artifacts	1			
Provide instructions	1			
Perform travel	3			
Check into hotel	2			
Distribution: 1s	4			
2s	5			
3s	4			

Figure 91: A sample prioritization matrix for the travel example, with UX priorities indicated. Note the even distribution of scores for the tasks.

Knowledge Design

Figure 92: Map of the New York City area showing the 3 main airports relative to Manhattan.

- New York's LaGuardia Airport is closest to the destination, but would require Pat to take a bus, which will be ugly at rush hour.

- Even though it is in New Jersey, Newark Airport is close enough to be a viable option, but requires taking a train to New York City and making a cumbersome transfer to the subway to get to midtown.

- JFK airport is the best option. Pat can take a train from the airport and make an easy transfer at the Jamaica train station to the E subway. It should take only a few minutes to taxi from the Lexington and 53rd Street E subway station to the hotel. This trip might take about an hour in total.

- Pat would need to land no later than 5:30 p.m. Pat's profile indicates that they prefer nonstop flights: Pat doesn't want to risk a plane change that could disrupt their schedule.

- There are a handful of nonstop flights from LAX to JFK on American Airlines, Delta, and JetBlue that arrive before 5:30 p.m. Our system can check which airlines still have first-class seats available and only present those options.

- Knowing Pat prefers to travel in style, and that they will have to get back to JFK the next day to fly home, the system suggests Concorde Hotel at 127 E. 55th St, just a few blocks from the restaurant, and close to the E subway station for the trip back to the airport.

- Our system offers Pat a few choices with clear timing and pricing. We show Pat how to get from the airport to the hotel, and later to the restaurant. Our smartphone app can integrate Google Maps and Google's Augmented Reality "Live View" walking directions to keep Pat from making mistakes. We tell Pat how to use Apple Pay or Google Wallet to pay for the subway.

Task-Oriented Design

Think of the system as the travel agent and identify which steps can be accomplished by the system.

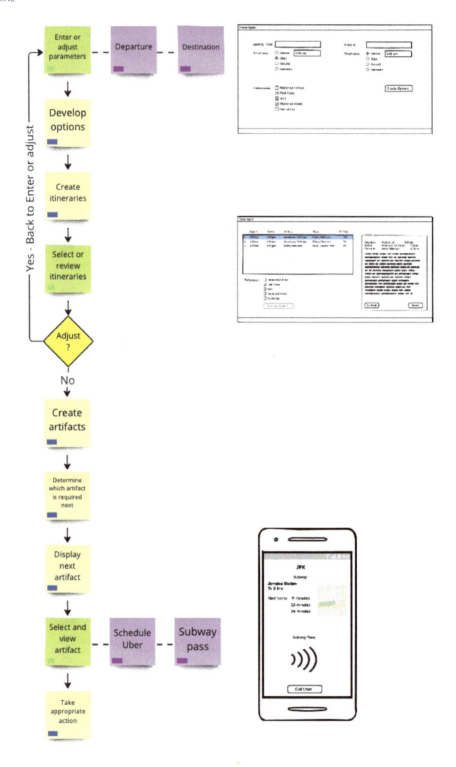

Figure 93: The optimized travel example task flow (described previously) with associated screen designs for the User (green) sticky notes in the task flow.

The simplified example of the travel task flow, Optimized:

- **User:** Enter or adjust parameters. **Artifact:** Departure, Destination.

- **System:** Develop options.

- **System:** Create itineraries.

- **User:** Select or review itineraries.

- **Decision:** Adjust? **Yes:** back to Enter or adjust parameters. **No:** go to next step.

- **System:** Create artifacts.

- **System:** Determine which artifact is required next.

- **System:** Display next artifact.

- **User:** Select and view artifact. **Artifact:** Schedule Uber, Subway pass.

- **System:** Take appropriate action.

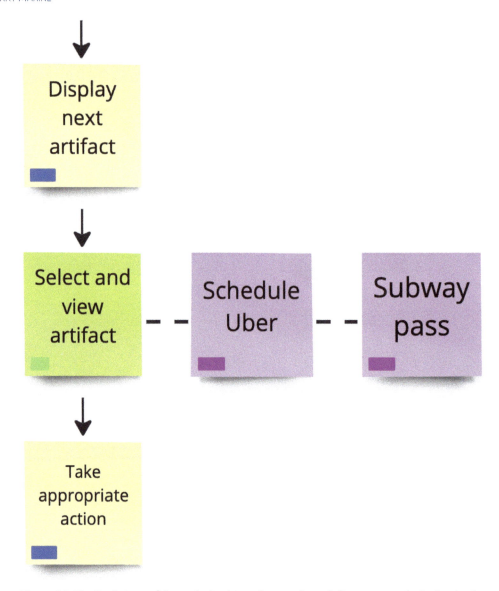

Figure 94: The final steps of the optimized travel example task flow to start designing backwards.

Final Steps Simple Travel Task Flow, Optimized:

- **System**: Display next artifact.
- **User**: Select and view artifact. **Artifact**: Schedule Uber, Subway pass.
- **System**: Take appropriate action.

Figure 95: A rough smartphone wireframe for one of the last steps of the travel example task flow. It includes a map with directions to the subway, time before the next trains leave, and a way to pay for the subway ride from the phone. It also has a button to call for an Uber ride.

Figure 96: A wireframe of the itinerary selection screen of the travel example. It lists the possible itineraries (with a description of the selected itinerary), and allows the user to set travel preferences, such as First class, Wi-Fi, rental car, etc.

To generate this itinerary, the system will need to capture various travel parameters as illustrated on the following screen:

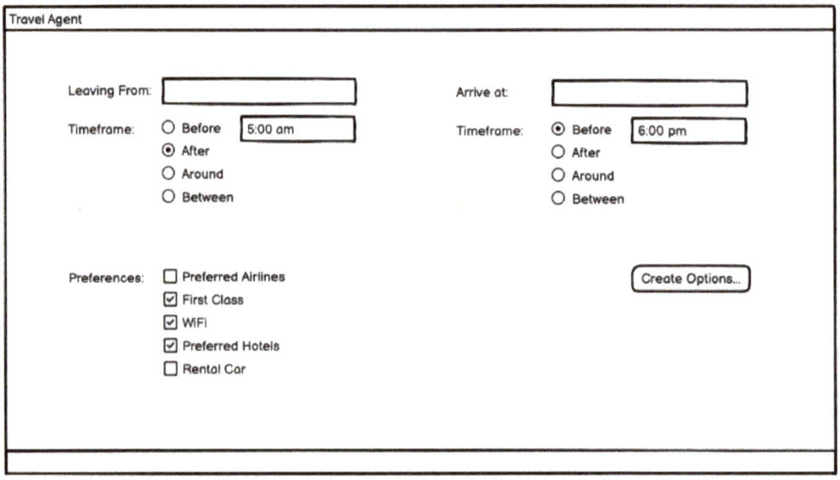

Figure 97: A wireframe of the starting point of the travel example task flow. This presents entry fields so the user can set departure and arrival times and locations, along with their travel preferences.

Keep in mind that this is not intended to be a perfect solution at this early stage, but it should capture the design strategy enough to conduct some low fidelity usability testing.

The following illustrates how the screens map to the flow diagram where there are green sticky notes representing user actions:

Usability Testing

Test tasks:

- Identify your starting or origin location.

- Identify your final destination and desired time to arrive.

- Indicate specific travel parameters such as a first-class flight, Wi-Fi on the plane, rental car not required, etc.

- Review itinerary options the system provides.

- Using travel artifacts (subway pass, room key, etc.).

- **Test Scenario:** You are Pat, an executive currently in Los Angeles (LA) for a client event. You just learned that you need to be in New York City (NYC) the next evening... [the rest of the scenario here].

- **Test Task 1:** What does the system use as the default the starting point for this trip? The address of your last known location (such as the hotel you are currently staying at), your current location (such as the coffee shop you are currently in), or does it require you to enter a location?

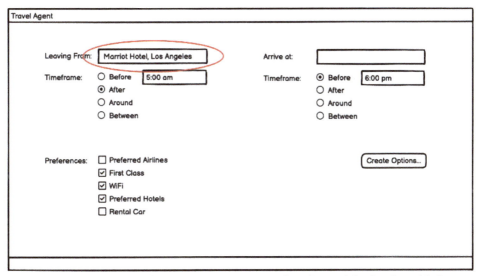

Figure 98: The travel example screen to enter current location and destination with Current location highlighted to show "Marriott® Hotel, Los Angeles" prefilled in the entry field. The red oval is for illustrative purposes, to show which field this task is referring to. Don't include such a highlight on the prototype screen.

- **Test Task 2:** Does the system accept general locations for the final destination, such as a hotel name, or does it require a specific address?

- **Test Task 3:** Do you need to indicate specific options such as first class, Wi-Fi, etc., before, after, or both when searching for available itinerary choices?

- **Test Task 4:** Does the system add a whole new itinerary if you change your final destination to a hotel brand in midtown Manhattan, NYC, or just update an existing itinerary?

- **Test Task 5:** If you suggest a 10:00 a.m. start time, does the system alert you that it will not get you to NYC in time for dinner?

Travel Example Summary

You may have noticed that many specific details were left out of the artifacts of this example project, such as in the task flows, user knowledge profiles, screen design, etc. That was intentional. The objective was to prompt you to start thinking in new ways and then let you take it from there.

This travel example illustrates how the knowledge-oriented design process flows and how the artifacts are connected, each informing the next step of the process. Moreover, it provides a real-world instance of how the process can more accurately define the problem and drive unique and better solutions.

www.ingramcontent.com/pod-product-compliance
Lightning Source LLC
Chambersburg PA
CBHW041007050326

40690CB00029B/5288